KEEP YOUR HEAD DOWN

*This account of our adventure is dedicated to
Leading Diver
Charles Smithard MID and Able Seaman Diver
Taff Rees,
who came back home with us but whom we were
never to see again;*

*to my father, the late Commander J.M. Bruen
DSO, DSC, RN, whom I miss;*

and to the forgotten men of the Falklands War.

CONTENTS

Foreword		ix
Prologue		xiii
Chapter 1	Preparations and Leaving	1
Chapter 2	Into Action	24
Chapter 3	A Busy Peace	100
Appendix 1	The War Reports	143
Appendix 2	The People	151
Appendix 3	The Cabaret	158
Appendix 4	A Career Remembered	167
Appendix 5	The Notebook	195

FOREWORD

by Vice Admiral Sir Donald Gibson KCB, DSC, JP, RN.

The author's father was my much admired and greatly loved commanding officer in a World War Two Fleet Fighter Squadron, a diffident hero with a well earned DSO and DSC. Diffidence is not the outstanding quality of his son, but the book resounds with his personal modesty and generosity towards others.

We always produce outstanding leaders in a crisis, and here is a new sort with his team, Charlie, Piggy, Jock 1, Rex, Dave, Wheels, Taff R., Buster, Tommo, Joe, Taff H., Jock 2, Chas, John Boy, and Whisky. They shared everything, all usually unwashed, hungry. They shared what little booze there was around, their leader entertained them with his fiddle and his poetry. When not in contact with unexploded armed bombs or mines they shared the common domestic chores, the humping of wet sandbags, and the tender care of the wounded on both sides of the conflict. They shared their makeshift accommodation, the leader sleeping in the lavatory, they shared the cold and discomfort, and they shared great professional pride.

I am not much of a man for poetry but I loved the poems in this book, which so much enhance the narrative, and are part of a depiction of a new style of leadership based on a unique personality, personal example, courage, high endeavour, with an intimate comradeship only possible when a small, highly professional team is up against it in war.

Well done Bernie, Charlie, Piggy, Jock 1, Rex and all the

rest. Bernie has written with great pride, not about himself, but about all of you.

Nonetheless, it is not suprising that senior officers, of more conventional mould, sometimes took fright when they saw you lot coming.

Donald Gibson

ACKNOWLEDGEMENTS

I should like to give particular thanks to:

Ron and Jaquie Harrison and Lieutenant Jeremy Hunt, Royal Navy, the computer experts who gave me so much help in producing this book; and to Commander Ian Shea of the Royal Navy of Oman, whose encouragement made the whole thing possible.

Thanks also to Lieutenant Commander Alan Malcolm, Royal Navy of Oman, and Mr Rory Allen BA (Hons.) Engl.Lit., M.Sc., who acted as proofreaders and commentators, Risail Photo Laboratories, who managed to reproduce the photographs from prints after somebody had 'borrowed' the negatives; and Surgeon Captain Rick Jolly OBE, Royal Navy, for his advice and assistance throughout.

AUTHOR'S NOTE

Dated and indented paragraphs are reproduced as written day by day in either the War Journal or the Notebook. These lived in the top left and right pockets of my combat jacket throughout. Entries were made whenever time was available, sometimes as things happened, sometimes later. Inevitably there are many gaps, but much of what is missing is covered by the accompanying text. Information in square brackets has been added by way of clarification and comment. These daily jottings reflect what was believed to be true at the time. They have not been corrected or updated. Some names have been left out to save embarrassment.

PROLOGUE

Yes mate, this is Falkland. You'll find a sangar over there. Air raid? Well, any minute really. You'll hear the whistle – if it goes. Yes, we've got Rapiers all around but I hear they're running out of petrol. No, keep your weapon with you. You may need it if you see one coming in. Food is at dawn and dusk, across that stone-field and bog. Yes, it is remote, isn't it, but the other got taken out by a 500-pound bomb. Just four dead. We were lucky really. Ten minutes earlier and they would have got the whole dinner queue. That Corporal Chef is good but he won't let you eat near his tent. Not surprising really. Hot water? Well, don't touch that lot, it's for the hospital. There's not a lot about, just scrounge what you can. Yeah, that's the hospital. God, those boys work hard. They haven't lost a case and I've seen some of them that came in. We all help out with the stretchers and at busy times. The Navy lads, the Divers there in their fort, they were up all last night with the casualties. They're OK. You'll know the helos bringing 'em in – they don't waste time landing and you can see them coming coz they burn a white light. That lot? They're going to a funeral. Four fly-boys shot down. And them – they're Argies. Yeah, they don't look too happy, do they! The Navy blew up a UXB on the beach yesterday. No one told them. It looked like a squall hitting a field of ripe corn, the way they took cover. But they're a sorry lot really. No idea of looking after themselves and young too. We do the best we can and sometimes you see them raise a smile. Not often though. What do they eat? Left over compo mostly. Well, we're short ourselves, they get what's left and they're grateful. Yes, that frigate's always there now, since the bombing that is. Right inshore like that – never anchors. They go out at night but are back by first light. I'd sure like to get over there for a bath and dhobi and a beer. There's none here. Mind you, the medics manage to get plenty of booze, but they need it. We don't grudge them that.

See you. Keep your head down!

BB
Rose Cottage
Fort Thompson
Red Beach
San Carlos
F.I.
12.6.82

THE VIEW FROM THE EDGE

Peering from a landing craft stuck in the kelp,
Watching an air raid filled with Rapier flares,
Ducking as the bullets flatten overhead;

Scrutinizing tension in a cable hoist,
Contorting, wrestling with a thousand pounder,
Waiting for the 'click' of its fuse 'going live';

Squinting at the brightness of molten metal
Showering from the bulkhead being cut away,
Wetting down the weapon to put out the flames;

Glimpsing the underside of a plane at dusk
Shrieking low over the hospital building,
Hearing its bombs detonating all around;

Seeking a route through a twisted skeleton,
Swinging above the smoulder of shipborn fires,
Hefting weighty explosives in a backpack;

Scanning bulkheads glowing in a burning ship,
Feeling explosions stagger the hull beneath,
Covering a body welded to the deck;

Finning backwards in a breaking wave at sea,
Fending off a mine, a beachball in the surf,
Recoiling from the horns that one must not bend;

Reaching, later, in among its circuits, while
Viewing the stillness of the Falkland evening,
Musing on the detonator – right or left?

Here and here the limits are,
Here the unknown is revealed.

It is the view from the edge.

1

Preparations and Leaving

4.5.82 Tuesday
Left Ma bravely this morn and arrived at HMS *Drake* [Naval Establishment at Devonport]. Sorted lift to Portsmouth with Clearance Diving Team. Haircut. Purchased flat hat. On to Fids's [Fiddler Jennings, my mentor and friend and a renowned musician]. Down to Swan [Harry Hartop's wonderful drinking establishment that was our HQ in Devonport]. Repositioned giant White Ensign in corner of bar.

Fiddler and I arrived at the Swan Hotel early. I had arranged to meet the Devonport 'Guzz-team' divers, who were due to form part of Fleet Clearance Diving Team Three, here and await the transport that was to take us to Portsmouth. Whilst waiting, we helped put up a giant White Ensign (that must have come from an aircraft carrier at least, it was so big) around two of the inside walls of the pub. Completing the task, we stood back to admire our handiwork. At this point a customer walked into the bar, ordered a pint of Hick's Special Draft ale (HSD, otherwise known as 'High Speed Death' or 'Old Mother Wormold's Dynamite Cough Cure and Worm Eliminator') and told the landlord that he did not think much of our efforts. The pub fell silent and all eyes turned. When asked why not, he rejoined that it would play havoc with the passing trade.

'How come?' inquired the nonplussed publican.

'Well,' came the answer, 'you'll get no Argies in here, mate!'

As the pub dissolved into laughter Ginge, one of the Plymouth Divers, entered.

'Boss, transport's here.'

And indeed, there stood a blue-light, red-wing Bomb Disposal Land Rover with the 'boys going south' climbing out of it.

'A parting glass,' said Fiddler, and presented each man with a tot.

'Rum for the lower deck, and for the wardroom. . . .' passing me a tumbler, ' . . . . gin. The Queen, God bless her!' Raising our glasses, we replied in like fashion and drained them dry. The adventure had begun.

Later, at a Little Chef, we stopped for a meal. I never pass the place now without remembering that moment and the sense of complete freedom I had. Everything was in order, my life had no loose ends to it and I could devote myself entirely to the task ahead. It was a wonderful feeling, almost like being born anew, and now everything that I had ever learned would be put to the test in the ultimate challenge.

Would you believe both Fids and I started recording silhouettes of 'downed' Argie ships/aircraft on the same day. Team arrived. Charlie, Phil, and Ginge (driver). Gave Fids my old yachting cap for safe keeping. Farewells. Off. Amusing journey down to HMS *Vernon* [the Alma Mater of the Diving Branch – probably the friendliest Naval Establishment in the Portsmouth area; renowned for its 'teas']. Welcomed like long lost son by Mr McShee the Hall Porter. Same old cabin, No 26.

It was while the four of us from Plymouth were ashore in the 'King and Queen' that we learned the news of the loss of HMS *Sheffield*. This was, of course, a great shock but I wait for the casualty reports. We also heard of the Harrier that was shot down and the pilot killed. Well, Donald [Vice-Admiral Sir Donald Gibson KCB, DSC,

RN; wartime colleague and great friend to my father, and lifelong friend and adviser to myself] said yesterday that we should expect some casualties soon, as we could not keep up the one-sided destruction for much longer. But the *Sheffield*! Well, they can stand by now, them Argies.

Did not ring Fiddler tonight. Turns out that Healey [Labour Defence Minister] would only let them have £20m instead of £40m to build *Sheffield* and consequently she was 40ft shorter and minus a complete weapons system. And he has the gall to point an accusing finger at the present Government!

5.5.82 Wednesday
Team mustered this morn. Spoke to them quickly before interviews with 1st Lt, Commander and Captain. He was most interested in Father [Commander J. M. Bruen DSO, DSC, Royal Navy; Fleet Air Arm fighter 'ace' of Second World War] being an aviator himself. All very helpful, as was Superintendent of Diving, Cdr Worsley. Everything is moving now and the latest buzz is that we may sail in QE2 down south.

At 16.30 we went to 4hrs notice. We were lacking much gear at that stage and efforts were now strenuously applied to get all ready, collected and packed ready for weighing as soon as possible. It seems an impossible task, especially in view of the fact that everyone in the Dockyard and Naval Base has gone home.

By 2100 we had about all we could get, but still unable to weigh and finish as we were short of [diving] gas, engines, arctic clothing and explosives. So we packed up for the evening and waited for FCPO George Sissons to arrive from Northwood. However, we were arranged to strip *Vernon* of everything they possessed at the 'GO' signal.

Saw Tony Coverdale in the Mess [Nuclear Submarine Engineer adept at inventing Emmett-like machines and playing the squeezebox]. As happy and full of fun as always. Had a couple of pints and a tune with him before going to the Chiefs' Mess to wait for George Sissons [Warrant Officer Diver of great renown, and one of the Diving Branch's 'men at Northwood' at the time].

He never actually turned up but we communicated at 01-ish [1 a.m.] and it seems 'we'm OK for until tomorrow'.

5th May 1982
Wednesday
HMS Vernon

Yer Fiddler,

All is in turmoil here as we have come from 48 hours NTM to 4 hours NTM [NTM: Notice to Move; the amount of time allowed for getting ready, before the actual command to go is given. Needless to say, every hour of NTM is precious]. So we are frantically packing all the gear we have just unpacked. Not a lot more I can say really. I'll bring you back a penguin.

I found the enclosed in my pocket [gold boxing medal] and would rather you hang on to it for me until I return.

See you around.

Bernie

P.S. The men are in good heart.

6.5.82 Thursday
By 1030 just about everything was top line, except the engines have not yet arrived [outboard engines for the Gemini inflatable boats, the platforms from which diving takes place]. At that point we were called forward and now it is a race against time.

By 1500 we were ready but the signal was not completed until 1600, 23½ hours after coming to 4 hours notice to move. Not bad for a day and a half. We have 4 chacons, 1 pot, 1 det tank, 16 hampers and 9 pallets of gas. The whole weighing 36,023lbs. Good work by the Team.

[**Chacon**: Chatham Container; the Royal Navy's versatile and long-lived bulk storage and movement system. Each container is about 10ft long by 5ft wide by 6½ft high, made of wood, strengthened with steel and with a double opening door at one end. The Chacons were the forerunners of the now universal commercial containers, and whoever designed them certainly got it right. **Pot**: Diver's slang for a decompression chamber. This one-man chamber has been the mainstay of diving support in the RN for many years. Air portable and self-contained, it is a wonderful piece of kit. **Det. Tank**: a steel tank, 3ft square, used for the storage of detonators. Explosives and ancillary gear travelled in their own boxes. **Gas**: various mixtures of oxygen and nitrogen used in Clearance Divers' Breathing Apparatus – specialist underwater equipment, non-magnetic and silent, used for bomb and mine disposal and 'attack swimming'.]

Sort of half-a-team run ashore this eve. Nothing to write home about. Short sitrep to Fids,

'Travelling, Keep to yourself, Address on way. Gone-me.'

20 killed in *Sheffield* and 24 wounded are serious. This is less than was feared and mainly consists of catering staff.

7.5.82 Friday

The latest 'Buzz' from Fleet ['rumour' from Commander-in-Chief Fleet at Northwood] this morning was, 'We know where you are going and we know how, but we cannot tell you yet.'

All day it's been 'Go! – Don't go!'

The lads did some recognition work in the afternoon and then were allowed ashore for the bank. I spent the afternoon filling up 'Will' forms. So that's done. Tobacco issue and last minute stores. By 1730, having heard nothing, I rang Fleet and got the message – 'Probably tomorrow or Sunday.'

So, lads allowed ashore this eve. On return to the Mess, saw a signal from midday saying that they wanted us on the *QE2*. That would be nice.

Quiet evening, really. Helped out behind the bar when the Retired Naval Officers' Association invaded. Watched TV. Waited.

In the afternoon I had a visit from a strange man who looked like your original absent-minded professor. He informed me that the Argentinians had so many of such-and-such a type of sea mine and that number of another type. I was most impressed by his accurate information and, although unsure of his precise position in the scheme of things, was aware that he must be something to do with the Intelligence Services. I complimented him on his detailed knowledge and asked how he knew just what the enemy possessed.

'My dear fellow, we have the receipts.'

8.5.82 Saturday
Still at 4hrs notice. Managed to go shopping for small travelling bag, flask etc. £80 or more! So what! Around midday found that we would not go today *bi-kul-takid* [Arabic for 'in all probability'] so I went (walked) to North End (and back) to see an excellent movie, *Gallipoli*. Stuart Aitkin's brother married at *Vernon* today. Saw Stu briefly [contemporary from Britannia Royal Naval College, Dartmouth, and a fine boat handler]. To bed early, except for being dragged out on a couple of occasions to answer telecons from Northwood [Commander-in-Chief Fleet]. Seems we will be embarking in the Trawlers from 'A' Island [Ascension Island] on 12th. One signal arrived at 0300 in morning.

9.5.82 Sunday
Had the lads up at Horsea today [Horsea Island; a man-

made lake originally used for testing torpedoes and now the Royal Navy Diving School, 'loved' by every Diver] for a dive and then two runs with the telegraph pole – obstacle type. First run 15 mins – 2nd run 8½. They were a bit hacked off by it until I showed them how they had been working better as a team the second time [a standard leadership ploy when welding together a group of people into a viable team in a short time – give them something to complain about, but make it something worthwhile].

Later in the afternoon we got our flight times. Tomorrow evening we fly out to Ascension Island to join 5 trawlers for what could prove to be a sick-making trip to the South Atlantic. Not looking forward to that or the inevitable watchkeeping involved. Still – it's war. Speaking of which, add ⛴ and 🚁 to the list of Argie losses. One trawler, one helo *Ilhamdulillah* [Arabic expression of rejoicing]!

Watched John Mills in an excellent short play on TV before retiring for a well-dreamed sleep.

10.5.82 Monday

This morning, while waiting for Dockyard Transport (for the gear) which was late, re-sorted the hampers, so now everyone has his own. The lads managed to drop the Det tank! No explosion, thank goodness. I lost my Secret signals; put them down in the Land Rover which promptly drove off to Portland [Naval Sea Training Establishment for the Fleet]. L/S Kearns dispatched to find them, which he managed to do. Met Jimmy Green (now L/S [D], ex-*Gavinton* and ex-mess-man.) Wished me good luck and parting words were, 'Keep your head down.'

Also strong message from Captain Oxley [Captain of HMS *Vernon*], 'Tell the team to come back safe and we will be thinking of them.'

From the Commander, 'We'll have a party when you get back.'

Everyone wishes us well and the lads are eager for the off. Goodbye *Vernon* – it has been fun.

'Will the last man leaving *Vernon* please turn out the light and shut the door.'

After problems getting all the diving gas away (like there was too much for one truck) we ourselves left around 1545, stopping at Newbury briefly so I could get Joe Gofton a harmonica. All met up again at RAF Lyneham, where we had a good meal. The flight was delayed from 2300 to 0410, which annoyed Hamish Lowden [Lieutenant-Commander Hamish Lowden, who ran the Northwood-end of the Branch organisation; he is of fame in the Branch, particularly for his equine accomplishments], who had come from C-in-C Fleet to see us off, and prompted him to have a go at the RAF. He gave the lads a brief, a good one, saying that this was a dangerous job they were going to and wishing all luck. After a brief crash-out [sleep; naval slang left over from my days as a trainee pilot] in the transit 'hotel' and an early breakfast, we flew out just after 0400. The lads have managed to crash-out on the racked gas bottles [as did I] and deck and generally the flight is not at all bad, if somewhat lengthy.

During the flight we were issued with bag meals and fruit squash in little cardboard cartons. The aroma of the crew's hot meal being prepared in the galley pervaded the aircraft and set mouths watering. Somehow the sandwiches, which seemed to consist of pink blotting paper in between compressed cardboard, did not taste quite so good after that. However, help was at hand and a treat in store. I managed to persuade the Load Master to allow us a couple of cups of near-boiling water, and with this initiated the magical transformation of two pot-noodles into a feast, albeit a small one, for the 18 of us. It took the edge off things a bit and helped draw us all a little closer together.

All in all, we were travelling light. The Team had mustered six days earlier, ostensibly 'just to get things together in case you are needed at a later date': such was the brief from Northwood. Consequently each man had brought only a 'steaming kit' of: a set of Action Working Dress (those light blue shirts and dark blue trousers that sailors wear), a set of civilian clothes and a normal change of underwear etc. for a couple of days. To these had been added a set of Combat Clothing (disruptive pattern camouflage), a set of 'arctic' underwear that would have fitted King Kong (one size only), 'arctic' socks (probably the best kit around) and personal diving gear. The sleeping bags, the only ones available, must have been designed for tropical pygmies. They were small-size and labelled 'Hot Weather' and ended around the chest. Well, you take what you can get. One thing I had insisted upon was that each man had a convertible camp-bed-cum-hammock.

Of all the kit that we could not bring, I most regretted leaving behind the five boxes of bomb and mine disposal tools that are the envy of every other service. I had been told that we would not need them, that they might be needed elsewhere, and that therefore we could not take them with us. This made me uneasy, but it was considered that the only bomb-disposal work that we were likely to encounter would be the occasional stray unexploded mortar bomb. How wrong can you be?

11.5.82 Tuesday
In the evening we arrived at the red-brown lump of volcanic debris that is Ascension Island. Very little grows here, and the island is made up of volcanic dust and rubble. Green Mountain, however, is the result of earth imports and has a farm built by the Royal Marines, as were most of the old buildings on the Island. The barracks are in the old colonial style and the Georgetown Jetty warehouse is truly magnificent, at one time the largest, un-centrally-supported roof in the southern hemisphere.

There seemed to be much confusion as to where we were to go and we ended up in the trawlers for the night. [The trawlers were 'ships taken up from trade' or 'STUFT' ships (as in a popular saying of the time: 'Want to fight a war? Get STUFT!'), which would be used by our forces to great effect, and with gallantry, for minesweeping and other activities.] Most in *Pict*, in which I know both Captain and 1st Lt, and some in *Northella*. I visited Martin Holloway [Lieutenant-Commander RN, Mine Clearance Diver and Senior Officer of the Minesweeping Squadron] in *Cordella* and had a couple of welcome beers.

Very hot evening/night onboard.

12.5.82 Wednesday

Went ashore early-ish. Lieutenant Alan Rankin (MCD-Ops Officer to the Squadron) sorted out who to go to, and off I went. Met with a strange, sort of 'we don't want to know you' attitude from Cdr at Ops, but despite this minor puzzlement managed to arrange for the ferrying of all our gear onboard *Sir Bedivere* by mid-afternoon [RFA *Sir Bedivere*; a Landing Ship Logistic (LSL) in whom we travelled South: sister ship to *Sir Galahad*, *Sir Lancelot* and *Sir Tristram*], using Seaking and Chanook helos. The lads arrived from the trawlers during the afternoon. They have to sleep on campbeds or in 'micks' down the messes [mick: sailor's term for a hammock] as there are no bunks or locker spaces available to them. Not the most comfortable of conditions.

The Royal Navy has produced a versatile piece of kit that can be either a campbed or a passable hammock. We had taken the precaution of procuring one of these for each man in the belief that they might prove useful. Not many of today's sailors have ever slept in a hammock, and Piggy (CPO (D) G. Trotter, my 2i/c) and I had to pass on much folklore and wrinkles regarding the subject. As the boys found out later, there is no place as comfortable as a 'mick' in a capful of wind and a rising sea-way.

As we progressed further and further south and the weather became more contrary, many of our lads' messmates craved the use of the things, if only for one hour's respite from the movement to which they were so unused. The Divers made up the watch of night-time lookouts on the bridge. Coming off watch straight to a gently swaying hammock must be the finest of experiences to the sailor, but it is one that few have known in these more modern days.

An emergency drill at dusk proved that the Ship's Company are not really taking this thing very seriously, despite the fact that we are putting to sea for the night, due to Argentinian submarine threat. Had a few beers in the mess tonight before turning in next to my sea-survival kit:

>   overalls
>   pullover
>   gymshoes
>   knife
>   water
>   immersion suit
>   woolly hat
>   gloves
>   torch
>   fiddle

13.5.82 Thursday
A very quiet and comfortable night in the four-berth cabin I share with 3 × RM Lts. Some movement on the ship, especially as we approach 'A' Island for anchorage. The lads slept on the flight deck last night. Took a long time to anchor, but did so by 1030. In the afternoon the lads got down the tank deck [upper deck stowage area where our gear and chacons had been off-loaded and chained down] and, amid much moaning (well, some – not much), got one 1/2 (1 + 1/2) chacons unpacked and

CDBA bottles out [Clearance Diving Breathing Apparatus; the bottles have to be hand-pumped and filled with oxygen and nitrogen mixed in the correct proportions, depending upon the depth required: it is handy to have a few ready at all times]. Also diving knives for the survival kits. Some FP [fiddle practice: the first piece of kit I packed was my fiddle, in its camouflaged case] in the FX [fo'c's'le; forward part of the ship] so as not to disturb watchkeepers. A movie in the evening. A bad Western.

14.5.82 Friday
Sailed at 0700 for the Falklands and the Task Force. Refuelled with one of the Tides (A75) at the start [RFA refuelling tanker of the Tide-surge class] and then off south. Instructed the lads in RAS [replenishment at sea] etc., during the forenoon, and after lunch they made up buddy lines [communication and safety lines used by divers to signal to each other under water] while I made up a hammock for bad weather sleeping. The weather is very nice up here and, let's face it, can only get worse. I think this ship will roll a lot. We are not stopping for the Trawlers but pushing on at best speed.

The food is excellent and plentiful for us, though the lads would like a little more. There are nigh on 400 of them, RM, RE, RAF (some) and 4 RN gunners and 1 GI [i.e. Royal Marines, Royal Engineers, Royal Air Force (bomb disposal team), 4 Royal Navy gunnery ratings for the Bofors guns and a Gunnery Instructor Senior Rate].

Friday 14th May

Yer Fiddler,

After an eighteen-hour flight in a Herky-bird [Hercules transport], via Dakar (first time I've been there), we arrived at Ascension Island, a barren lump of volcanic debris, except for the Royal Marines' Farm on Green Mountain, planted over a hundred years ago on soil brought in by ships as part of their customs dues. I was most impressed by the barracks they built and the warehouse at Georgetown Jetty; the largest un-centrally-supported roof in the southern hemisphere for many a year, until recently.

Nobody actually knew where we were supposed to be going and so we were put on the five Hull Trawlers at anchor. I soon had this changed next day and had my Team transferred to RFA *Sir Bedivere* along with 36,000lb of our stores. After two days at anchor, the nights spent steaming because of Argy submarine threat, we finally set sail for the Falklands today. We were supposed to go in company with the Trawlers but that would have taken two weeks, so now we are travelling 'at best speed', all alone, to RV with the Task Force. There are all sorts onboard. A Company of Royal Marines, designated Battle Casualty Reliefs; an RAF EOD [Explosive Ordnance Disposal, i.e. bomb disposal] Team; Royal Engineers to build a Harrier airfield and 1 × GI plus 4 × RN Gunners to man the two Bofors guns which are our only defence against anything.

Fairly obviously our DC [damage control] state is high and we are darkened. Also we have had the ship's name boards and numbers painted out. The ship is fairly crowded and my boys, being late arrivals, are in hammocks, in with the Royals. Food is very good although not in great quantities, and generally everyone is quite comfortable. I think that most people will fairly soon be envying my Team their 'micks' when the rough weather begins. I have mine slung on the well-protected and heated-by-the-galley-exhaust Poop Deck. But for the nonce the weather is quite nice and very sunny. However, the Old Lady does give indications of rolling like a pig.

I have found myself a private hole to practise in [fiddle], and there is a Sod's Opera coming up soon. One of the Gunners has just come from the RN Display Team and is very adept at dancing the Hornpipe. So that looks like a good thing to do.

That is about it for now. I do not expect to be back in UK at least until September or October as there will be a great deal of work to do down there, especially after the end of hostilities. I'll keep you posted.

Bernie

Friday, 14th May
Ascension Island

Dear Ma,

If you have a look at the big Reader's Digest atlas in the study and open it to the Atlantic Ocean, you will see Ascension Island about half way down, between South America and Africa. Now, if you get out your magnifying mirror and look very closely at the south end of it, you should be able to see some people sitting on the beach waving at you. Well, that's us, our little team of stand-by divers.

We arrived here a couple of days ago and, not being needed, have been shoved aside to this rather splendid beach (but living in tents, which is rather fun) where we spend half the day working and the other half sun-bathing. It seems that the build-up, brilliant as it has been, was perhaps a little too rapid and they are rather over-stocked with divers. They're not going to send us back, though, because we might have to do a salvage job down in South Georgia. That will be quite amusing if it comes off and rather good for me as I missed the chance of an expedition there a few years ago. But more than that, to have gone from snow and ice climbing in Skye (57°N) to diving in S Georgia (55°S) in a matter of weeks would be, in itself, quite an adventure.

As to the activities in the Falkland Islands, everyone here

is quite confident that the Task Force will have that sewn up in very short order. All that rush and bustle in Portsmouth was exciting enough but now at least we have a chance to relax and get our gear sorted out. One of my 'Leaders', Chas, has just asked who I'm writing to and sends his regards. No, you haven't met him but, like the rest of the bunch, he's a good man. I'll tell you all about them when I get back.

I'll have to finish now. We are only allowed one of these free letters each every so often but I'll do my best to keep you informed of any interesting developments, if they happen. But now I think I'll have another beer and get my tan evened up a bit.

I hope Bruno-dog is behaving himself and all is well with you.

Love,
Nigel.

15.5.82 Saturday

Spent most of the day reading the Diving Manual and finding out how much I'd forgotten. Also had a couple of FPs, one with Joe Gofton on harps [musician's slang for harmonica or mouth harp]. He's just learning. PT in the evening really showed me how unfit I am. Like an old man. The circuit knackered me and it was only what I might have done as a warm-up before a full boxing circuit a few years ago.

RPC [Request the Pleasure of your Company; hence 'a cocktail party'] for the Ship's Officers before dinner. After, nothing much so turned in and dreamed of happier days at the White House when we were a family [home, before the death of my father in the late 1960s]. How long ago those days seem. Now the family unit has gone and we are three separate entities. I doubt it will ever return.

I had spent the last three years away from the Diving

Branch, first as Chief of Police on the remote island of Diego Garcia in the British Indian Ocean Territories (I had upset someone and was sent away to cool my heels for a year), and then seconded to the Sultan of Oman's Navy, as captain of the Fast Patrol Boat 'Al Mujahid', as the 1980 Gulf War started. Long patrols in the Strait of Hormuz do little for one's diving practice, and inevitably a certain amount of revision was required, particularly as I had been pulled off foreign service leave to form the Team.

Our expedition to cross the Hardanger-Jokulan ice cap in Norway had been cancelled, owing to the existing situation, and some members of that team had gone to Skye, hoping to find some snow and ice climbing in the Cuillins. Not a snowflake nor an icicle was to be found, and we returned early. Arriving at my mother's house, I received a message to ring a certain number at Northwood immediately. 'If you want to lead a team down south,' said the voice on the line, 'get here yesterday.' 'On my way,' said I, and without even having removed my rucksack I said goodbye to Ma and departed.

Now, here we were on our way, with as much equipment as we could muster in the short time available.

BEQUEST OF HONOUR

> I wonder what our fathers would have thought
> Could they have witnessed sons
> Trading on their sires' heroic deeds,
> With vehemence of pride,
> To heighten their small standing in the school?
>
> For though an undertaking thus discharged,
> With little thought for self,
> Changes one small section of the whole,
> So in translation can
> It cause the greater issues to unfold

Thereafter, as the years process in turn,
To reach along that span,
Growing weaker in its potency,
Yet able still to shape
The course of other actions by and by.

Thus did our fathers' exploits when at war,
Indexed by the ribbons
Proudly borne, bestow upon their heirs
Esteem and rank conferred
By rule-subjected schoolboy parallels.

How would they think if they could but observe
Those same, if fewer, sons
Take up mantles laid aside in peace
And, never doubting, stride
Away to earn authentic accolades?

16.5.82 Sunday
The weather has turned this morn and we are getting some movement in the Ship. However it is still fairly sunny. Put my 'mick' up on the poop deck for future use and was in it most of the day, alternating between the Diving Manual and HMS *Ulysses* (for the third time).

'Beasting' (RM's name for PT) from 0815-45 better today. Played fiddle for the church service, only about 30 people there, 6 from FCDT3 (1/3rd). Afternoon spent reading and FP on the frd end of Tank deck.

Film, *Dr Syn*, in the evening, which I found quite enjoyable. Crashed out in mick this night but woke at 0200 leaping [in pain]. Back bad so retired to cabin and bunk. Shame not to be able to sleep in a 'mick' any more.

It was amazing how much reading and study was required to bring myself back to speed in my specialisation. Like a great many things, you think you know it and will never forget it, but it is only when you want to recap that you realise just how much has slipped away. However, it soon comes back.

17.5.82 Monday
Found today that all the survival suits issued to us by the Dockyard have been slashed to useless. Incredible – someone should be hung! How could anyone send people to War knowing that the life saving gear is useless. Sent a signal of such to C-in-C Fleet, FO Portsmouth [Flag Officer Portsmouth] and *Vernon*. Bastards!

Took a reel of photos for C-in-C Fleet (the lads putting on their most pissed-off expressions) and we are packing up the suits for Superintendent of Diving. Most of the day spent reading and studying as the Booties are shooting on the Flight Deck. Very interesting lecture on the Falkland Islands in the Wardroom. PT in the evening, a good sesh. 27 mins non-stop. The press-ups are killing my back, though.

Quiet evening reading in the Mess. We are second in the Ship's Quiz so far with one day to go (the Embarked Officers, that is).

Sea is really quite flat today and the sun shining. We now have a Bofors [Bofors 40mm anti-aircraft gun; these ones were dated 1942 – still good though] mounted on each side of the FX and they are improvising double LMG [light machine gun, of the Bren gun ilk] mounts on Tank and Flight Deck – 4 in all. Plus a further 4 single LMGs at strategic points. Today the lads have been inflating Geminis and pumping gas. [Gemini rubber boats are inflated by a foot pump. Breathing gas is pumped from large storage bottles to the small working bottles by two men on a hand pump and one in the middle lending his weight to the effort: pumping gas is synonymous with 'getting fit'.] I've been doing the amendments [to the CBs or Confidential Books: mostly about bombs, mines and other explosive devices and how they work]. All of them. Phew!

A survival suit is designed to be of instant use when it is necessary to jump into the sea in the event of abandoning ship. Made of a light rubberised material, it is of such ample proportions that it is easy to put on, even in the dark and amid the inevitable confusion of such a situation. Once one is inside, the tapes at ankle, knee, waist and neck are tied tight, and one may jump overboard in the confidence that little, if any, water will enter the suit. Consequently one's chances of survival are greatly enhanced, particularly in the cold waters of the Antarctic.

As we drew nearer to the war zone, it became time to check that everyone in the Team was familiar with the dressing procedure and was sufficiently practised to be confident in its use. It was with very real concern, therefore, that we found, on opening the sealed packages, that not only were the arms and legs of the survival suits knotted, and the tapes already tied up tight, but the suits themselves had been slashed beyond repair. They say that if one's parachute does not work, one should return it and get another. We were in a similar, if one degree less terminal, situation. We could not use them. There were no usable spares. We had to trust to fortune. I expect that there were some ears burning in the Dockyard that day and, I hope, some very red faces when the culprits were called to account – if indeed they ever were. We heard nothing more at the time, but later discovered that the slashed suits were intended for parachute-drop test weights.

18.5.82 Tuesday
Woke up to an appreciable swell from the South West (on the head) after an uncomfortable night with the A/C switched off. PT OK this morning but Buster Mottram [Able Seaman Diver] buggered his back. I got the letters to C-in-C Fleet and SOD [Superintendent of Diving] typed and in the mail this morn [report on survival suits and a reel of film by way of illustration].

Weather coming from the West and causing some rolling. Excellent movie in the evening, *California Dolls*.

19.5.82 Wednesday
Weather worsening. Many sea-sick. Rolly Grant bad [Lieutenant, Royal Marines, one of four of us in a small cabin]. Not feeling too good myself in evening. Took pill – better. Could not stay on bunk due to rolling. Slept in passage until 0200 when wardroom empty, then moved in there among much flying debris.

20.5.82 Thursday
Ship rolling to 37° to starboard, less to port. Spent the morning reading – all activity suspended. Book – George R. Stewart's *Earth Abides* – for the 3rd time. At noon we entered the Roaring Forties. Had to slow down a bit. Finished *Earth Abides*. What an excellent book. In the evening the film *Waterloo*. Classic.

21.5.82 Friday
I know it's Friday 'coz we had fish for lunch. Slept very well on the deck until 0800. Getting dark later these days. Sea much calmer. Now down from Force 7 to Force 4. [The Beaufort Scale describes Force 7 as 'a moderate gale of 28-33 knots of wind: the sea heaps up and white foam is blown in streaks from breaking waves'. It advises fishing smacks to stay in harbour and those at sea to heave-to. Force 4 is described as a moderate breeze.] Read. Lunch. Studied mines. [We carried a collection of Confidential Books that gave us much information on the subject.] In the evening we learned of the bridgehead established on the Falklands and had a party. Singing mostly, though I did the 'Impossible Task', the 'Monaco Grand Prix' and played fiddle. [The first is an original recitation in the classic mode and can be found later in this narrative. The second is a Gazoo mime sketch I wrote that has to be seen and heard to be believed. Both of these bore much repetition and became firm favourites with everyone.]

Retired when Rugby songs were started at the shout. Slept on deck as enough rolling to throw me out of pit [bunk].

Very late, John Buchanan threw himself into the cabin, treading on me, after a sleeping David Lewis, and shouting/singing.

BB, from the deck, 'John! Thin-out!!'

'Sorry, Bernie.' and left.

Thereafter an uncomfortable night sliding around on the deck.

TASK FORCE

> They don't want us, they want our bodies;
> Need our talents, not ourselves.
> Conflict calls for dedication,
> Expertise enhanced by nerve.
> Now ascends the banished leader,
> Outcast of promotion's cull,
> Weaving spells of valour's mystic
> Vital whisper, 'Follow, all!'
> But do not bring your conscience,
> Do not bring your soul.
> The first you'll not be needing,
> The second will be stole.

22.5.82 Saturday

Learned of 1 Frigate sunk and 3 Harriers lost in the invasion but between 11 and 17 Argies shot down. Mood in the Mess one of determination, optimism and hope for few casualties. Apparently 3 RM dead so far.

Charlie's Birthday – 'Happy Birthday, Charlie.' The Team.

Emergency drills this morn with 'exercise fire' in engine room and 'rocket strike' on Chiefs' mess. Weather worsening, now up to about a 7 or 8 but from the bow; movement not too bad [fresh gale of 34 knots of wind, waves moderately high with crests breaking to spindrift;

smacks are advised to make for harbour (beyond this smacks are not advised at all – they're on their own)]. Now packed up for action. After lunch went up to the bridge for 2 photos of the weather. A classic force 8. waves marching regularly from the horizon, their surface covered in streaks of foam and their tops blown off into spume. Later the weather moderated and I got head down. In evening an RPC from Ship's Officers. 2100-2200, funny time! Everyone slept fully dressed tonight as we are close to the war and should be ready for all eventualities.

23.5.82 Sunday
Church this morn. Did some pre-church tunes, 'Barren Rocks' ['Barren Rocks of Aden'], 'Planxty Irwin', 'English Garden', 'Dark Isle'; and end church RM march out ['Life on the Ocean Wave']. Everyone packing battle kit. Our cabin full of bullets, guns and gear. This evening R/V'd [met up with] the Task Force. Helo [helicopter, chopper, paraffin pigeon, wocker-wocker, cab, toad-fish, etc.] alongside.

'Who are you?' then 'Proceed to next point.'

A great upsurge in morale in the ship and a feeling of relief at meeting the RN ships [Task Force]. Military Officers won the 2nd round of the Inter-messdeck Quiz. I wonder if there will be a 3rd round. Film in evening. Retired to bed fully clothed, as did everyone.

All gear packed ready for the off.

5 Mirage, 1 Skyhawk + possible 2, 2 Helos, 1 supply boat [day's total Argy losses as we heard them].

THE ACCOUNT

What do I have
To offer my Country?
My Services -
They are already bought.
My Loyalty -
But that is understood.
Duty – Honour -
Were they not always there?
My Enterprise -
Without it I am nought.
My Worldly Worth -
Would that I had to give.
Love of Country -
That was never questioned.

No. What I have
Is reckoned now to be
But a gesture,
An overkill: and yet
Despite the mock,
The denigrating words,
I have a Life
And that I volunteer.

No man can offer more.

2

Into Action!

WAR!

And in those days a tangled veil
Was drawn across the sky.
A madness, kindled in the sun
(Made Goblin there withal),
Convulsed and gibbered in its rage
To light inhuman pyres.

Now, squatting with a rancid grin,
This spawn of incubi
Bestirred the earth with turbulence,
Awoke a tainted squall
And conjured up the retching smoke
Of high explosive fires.

So, Demons, deep in artifice,
Bestow their gifts – supply
The oily dust to choke and burn,
But, in that reeking pall,
The Goblin meets a darker shroud
And, every night, expires.

(Written nine years later about the Gulf War, this piece is relevant to any conflict and the effect it has.)

24.5.82 Monday
Entered Falkland Sound about 0830. Anchored in San Carlos Bay 0940. I watched the entrance from forward lower, lower bridge. Silently the blacked out ships slipped by us, ahead two fires and smoke burned. As we got closer it became apparent that I was looking at a burning Type 21 Frigate. Aft of the bridge, the superstructure there was nothing but a bulkhead pierced by holes highlighted by the flames behind. The bridge was at a crazy angle and a 'charlie noble' [small funnel] remained amidships. Where the main compartments should have been in the superstructure there was just a nothing.

1320, watching the last throes of *Antelope*. She broke in half and with vasty smokes, the stern sank. The bow at 45°.

Around lunchtime, Brian Dutton, Boss of FCDT 1 [Lieutenant-Commander B. Dutton (MCD) RN; leader of the Fleet Clearance Diving Team, now labelled No. 1 of 5: we were FCDT No. 3] came aboard to find out about Bomb Fuses. Meeting between us and RAF B+MD [Flight Lieutenant Alan Swan; an experienced bomb disposal officer with a guitar]. Shortly after lunch we left in an LCVP [Landing Craft Vehicle/Personnel] to go to *Argonaut* where Chris Meatyard [Staff MCD officer to Commodore Amphibious Warfare] was looking at a bomb Brian's going to get rid of. Stopped at *Sir Galahad* to pick up some gear. Shortly after leaving, A/C warning Red [the warning of an immediate attack by aircraft]. Headed for shore in time to see mixed Argie Canberras [probably not Canberras in fact] and Mirages attack the LSLs [Land Ship Logistics; for this attack they had reversed their normal approach direction and had hit the ships in their supposedly 'safe' anchorage]. Saw one dodge over *Sir G* and drop bomb with great splash. No explosion. Later, as she swung, saw hole in stbd side where bomb struck, but UXB [unexploded bomb; this was probably *Lancelot*: *Galahad* was struck on the port side]. Crew ditching ammo off ship like crazy.

Two more A/C attacks and saw 2 Mirage go down. Blowpipe rockets [man-portable anti-aircraft guided missiles] and guns going off everywhere. One marine in the LCVP reckons he scored hits on a Mirage that came over us. Everyone cheered. *Antelope* slowly sinking. *Lancelot* being abandoned. We are stuck on the beach on a falling tide. I think I would prefer to be ashore rather than in a ship now.

Brian and I went to *Argonaut* to see Chris Meatyard, our 'tasker'. We found him just emerged from diving inside the shambles of the Sea Cat magazine where the latest UXB had lodged itself. Discussing the situation between us, we realised that we were the sum total of the Navy's bomb disposal force in the area and, unless something was done soon, and done by ourselves, we could soon have more problems than we would be able to handle. The explosion of the *Antelope* bomb had precluded any thought of rendering safe these weapons by fuse removal. The last attempt in that ship had gone horribly wrong and had torn the guts out of her. Thus, inevitably, came the question, 'Can you take the bomb out of *Galahad* without removing the fuse?'

This was a nice question to be asked because, in a perverse sort of way, here was bomb disposal, in the literal sense of the term, taken to its ultimate conclusion. In fact, being appreciative of this kind of twist, I was happy to apply myself to the situation. Now at last there was something to do, something that we would attempt by ourselves. We would stand or fall by our own efforts; an enviable situation to be in during hostilities.

We were also asked to move to the same ship as berthed FCDT 1 but, eggs in baskets, I prevailed upon Chris to put us ashore at Red Beach from where we could operate at night without constraining our host ship. They all sailed at dusk.

On to *Argonaut* where there is a UXB in the Sea Cat Magazine. Certain meetings with Chris Meatyard, SMCDO, interrupted by an air raid warning red, when Brian and I legged it ashore (again a question of 'eggs in baskets'). Later, back in *Sir B* for a late supper. Lads in good heart having got over the attacks this morning.

Bomb hit *Bedivere's* port yard, severed port crane cable (which dropped onto a very surprised Bofors crew) and passed through FX garden wall. Close!

FCPO Mick Fellows [2 i/c FCDT 1] on board after his epic bomb shift in another ship, having visited *Sir G*. [It had been reported that there was a UXB on board RFA *Sir Galahad*, and this was the first recce of this bomb.] One of my men was in a no-go state having seen the mess with him. Lost one there, I think. Not what one expects from a CD [Clearance Diver]. *Sir B* credited with one Mirage shot down. *Ilhamdulillah!*

Through the evening and into the morning of 25th worked on two UXBs in *Sir G* and *Sir Lancelot*. I have *Sir G*, Piggy has *Sir L*. Mine is in a lot of choss in the battery store port side. Piggy's in the centre of the superstructure. Hopefully unarmed. Packed in at 0400. Home at 0500. Up at 0700 with immediate Awkward. [Searching the bottom of a ship with divers is extremely awkward at times, particularly if you find the limpet mines you are looking for.] Over 1 hr to get ready but then search of *Sir B* and *Sir G*.

Check of *Sir G* and *Sir L* and visit to *Fearless* around dawn (1100!) then back to *Sir B* for much air-raid-interrupted lunch. Tried to sleep after but more raids and interruptions until order to move to *Intrepid* at 1530. 1630 heads down for 5th air raid.

Col Sgt Ginge (Royal Marine) arrived in an *Intrepid* LCT to take them there. (Old *Bulwark* acquaintance.)

The *Sir Galahad* bomb had made a terrible mess. Entering on the port side, below the shade-deck, it had punched its way through several compartments and, picking up an alloy bulkhead on its way, had bounced around the battery charging room before coming to rest amongst the havoc it had created. On this final madcap spree it had taken the liberty of smashing every carboy of acid in the place and had liberally scattered this and other mundungus around the compartment.

The bomb in *Sir Lancelot* had come to rest underneath a companion-way which led from the recreation space to the officers' accommodation on the deck above. The immediate area was used to store the ship's films. The weapon had insinuated itself tightly, nose up at 45°, beneath the lower treads of the stairs. Not easy to get at.

I went to have a look at the *Sir Galahad* job first. We knew very little about what we had there at this stage, but one thing was clear: we must have only one person around it at a time. Was it fitted with a time-fuse? If so, how long had we got? The first thing to do was to go and have a close look at it. Now, I had never seen a real live one before and, judging by the state of the compartment, I would not get to see much of this one either.

In such a situation, the first thing to do is to get used to the idea. Ten minutes spent just observing the creature from the doorway certainly helped. Now to enter the compartment and have a look from a different angle. Trying to get across such a space without actually touching anything is an interesting experience, and one which gives a whole new meaning to the expression 'walking on eggshells'. However, by moving slowly and by dint of hanging from every available pipe, channel-plate and ring-bolt on the deckhead, the other side was reached and a long look undertaken. There was an enormous amount of debris around that obscured any gainful view and it seemed that the Beast was saying, 'Leave me alone; I want to stay here.' At least, though, some of the initial mystique had now worn off and we had made contact. Time to make a quiet if somewhat ape-like exit, and go over to *Lancelot* to have a look at her visitor. When *Galahad* was abandoned that day, the ship's company had shut down everything and she was like a ghost ship: cold, dark, dead, echoing and clammy. *Sir Lancelot* was quite different.

We approached the darkened hull from the stern and found a wire rope-ladder hanging from the starboard winch-deck. Securing the Gemini to this, we climbed it and stealthily crept on board; except for the RAF bomb disposal Senior, who elected to stay where he was. Once on board, we became aware of a peculiar smell. Either this ship had been burning or it was just about to catch fire. We entered and soon found the source of the odour. The galley range had been left switched on and, although all generators had been shut down, the emergency motor was still running, producing power for the galley stoves and emergency lighting. On the range, a huge cauldron of bubbling fat was indicating by the noxious smoke it produced that it was just about ready to burst into flames. A quick flip of the switch to 'off', and that was the best day's fire prevention I'd ever done. The food cooking on the stove was too overdone to be edible, but we were presented with a welcome bonus when, on opening the oven, we discovered several large trays of jam tarts, all baked to perfection. Some of these we lowered to the Gemini, where our erstwhile companion from the RAF was endeavouring to keep warm.

Finding the UXB was not that hard. It had entered through the starboard side aft and, leaving a trail of destruction, had ended up in the cupboard opposite the Embarked Forces office. Following such a trail, expecting at any moment to discover the quarry hiding in the debris of aluminium sheeting, broken formica, smashed furniture and asbestos insulation, is guaranteed to sharpen the dullest wit, and it was with some relief that a voice was heard to sing out, 'Found it!' just as if we were taking part in a treasure hunt. Having ascertained the bomb's position, hunted around for any more and found none, we set to looking for gear that might help us in our efforts.

Piggy went to have a sit and a think in the office opposite. On the desk he found a bomb fuse, and under the fuse was an instruction manual which depicted the selfsame device. Here was a stroke of luck. This was the fuse removed from another ship's UXB a couple of days earlier by the two Army bomb disposaleers, just before their ill-fated call-out to *Antelope*, that ended so tragically. Perhaps they were even discussing this fuse when the call came. Now we could find out if the bombs were armed. If they were not, the removal would be relatively simple, but if they were armed, then we had a problem. These were not simple fore-and-aft fuses but ones that would actuate an explosion at the slightest movement. We had been asked to remove the UXBs from the ships and, after *Antelope*, not to attempt to take out the fuses. Could we effect that removal?

Here was a tricky situation, but one which, with a lot of care, could be solved by the application of pure seamanship. But that was for tomorrow.

Piggy and I decided that we would split our forces and tackle one bomb each. I would take three men and have a shot at the *Galahad* problem first. If that worked, he and his men would make an attempt at the other. If not – he would have a go anyway. Morning was now fast approaching and, as we had been told to work only at night, it was time for all good Divers to seek the protection of their own ship. Besides, our 'adviser' in the Gemini was getting very cold. We returned to *Bedivere*.

Tommo, Whiskey and Buster Mottram [Leading Seaman (Diver), Able Seaman (Diver), Seaman (Diver)] came with me to get out the *Sir G* bomb. Started at 2030, had it out by 0315. Had to take it out of a pile of gash, unwrap some alloy from around it, sling it first of course, and hoist two decks and outboard 20 ft. All accomplished with support from a *Fearless* stoker team (led by mother-hen-ish Cdr Engineer) and *Sir G's* Engine Room staff.

Worked well and we lowered it into a Gemini full of cornflakes to cushion the ride.

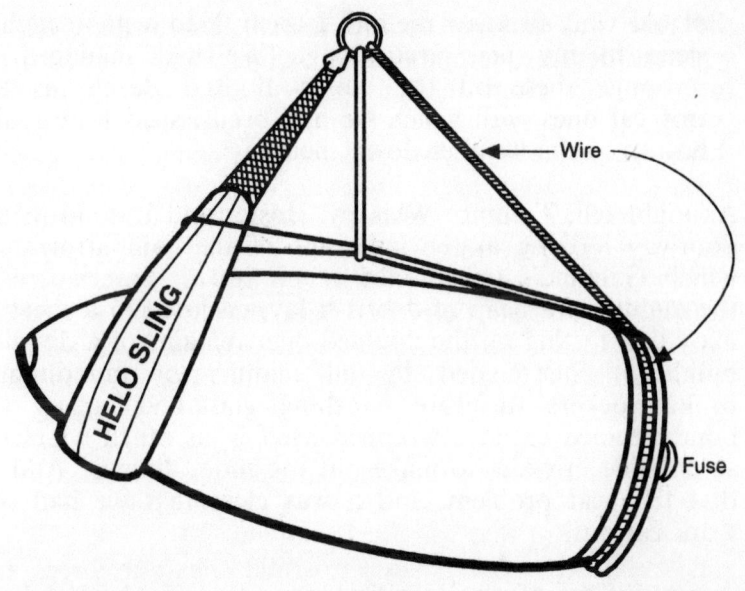

Tommo towed it out, slashed the Gemini, but as it would not sink finally had to roll the bomb over the side. Had a little party afterwards, also collected some gear. Then Piggy and I went to *Sir L* to have a go at his. This curtailed by a bombardment warning and us taken to Green Beach of all places, 7 miles away. Bloody cold. Eventually managed to get to *Intrepid* where they decided to send us ashore. Ginge's LCT had a hole in it so we had to dock up for repair. Getting a bit knackered now with little sleep for three days, however will survive. Must wash. Got an hour in and then entertained in the Sgts' mess for another. Eventually left for Red Beach and, after a 'brief' in *Fearless*, settled into a refugee existence in the BMA. [The hospital at Red Beach was set up in an abandoned refrigeration plant, built of cement-skimmed cork blocks in a steel frame, with a corrugated iron roof: very well insulated.] Teapot [a mate from Plymouth] turned up and Colin Healey [Captain RM] (ex *Bulwark*) plus several other Docs from of old who all knew me and I them. Had a good night's sleep in my new arctic bag. [We had managed to scrounge these off the Stores at Red Beach, as the tropical ones with which we had been issued were really not up to the weather down there.]

As night fell, Tommo, Whiskey, Buster and I stood in the doorway looking at the wreckage of the compartment in which Galahad's unexploded bomb rested. Somewhere in the middle of a heap of debris it lay, enclosed in a sheet of alloy and resting on the doubled-over remains of a dividing bulkhead. Surrounded by all manner of mundungus, broken lockers, furniture, panelling, glass and lagging, the bomb seemed to have wrapped itself in as much wreckage as possible in order to make our job more difficult. Add to that the acid problem, and it was clear that we had our work cut out.

Again, the most important first step was to look at and get used to the device and show the new team members how to move around the compartment – carefully. When all had thought through the implications of the task and were happy with the situation, preparation began. Tommo took charge of clearing a working area, within the compartment but not too close to the bomb. I went off to search for equipment to complete the task. By the time I had collected chain tackles, cordage, shackles and all sorts of other rigging gear and brought them to the scene of the crime, the three of them had cleared a space by the double doors, swept it clear of debris and even scrubbed out. We rigged lights and set about our task.

A piece at a time, we removed more and more of the debris, being most careful not to jar or scrape any other part of this giant, three-dimensional jigsaw. I was reminded of the child's game of 'pic-a-stic', except that here the sticks were bits of jagged metal or splintered wood. Slowly the pile grew smaller, until we could remove no more of it from where we were positioned. Every few minutes

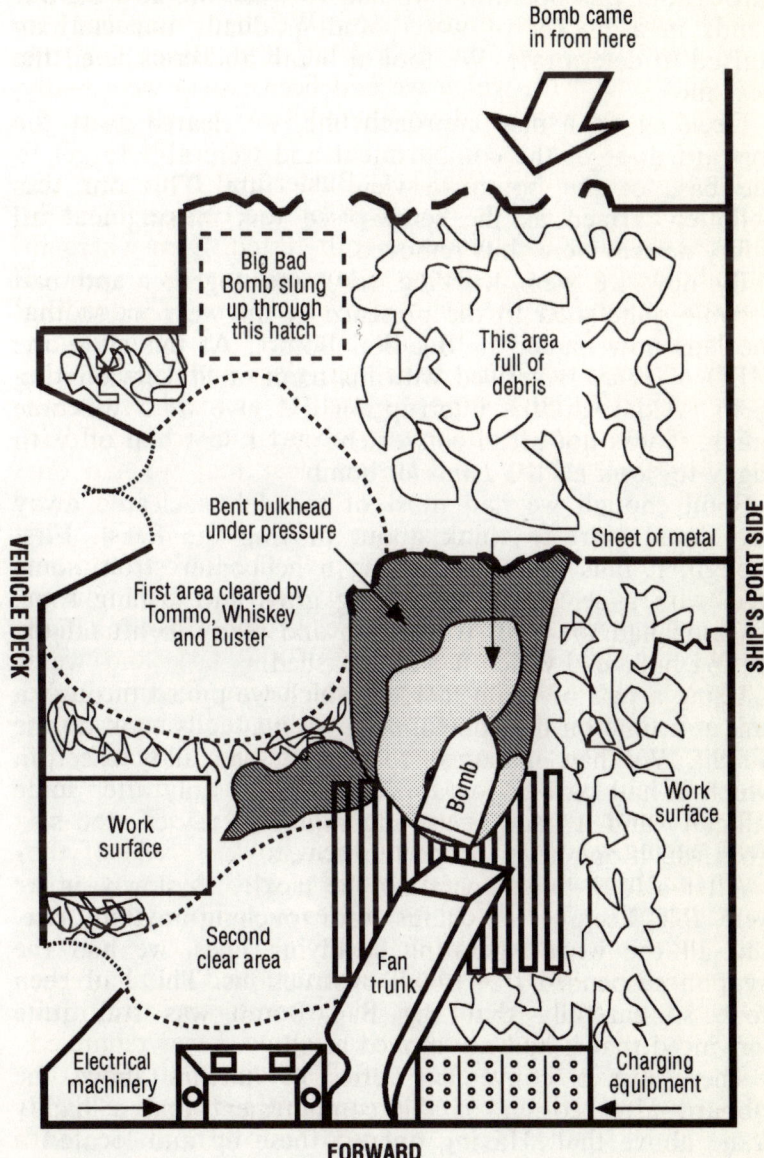

throughout this operation we had to wash the acid off our hands in a bucket of water, and gradually our clothing started to deteriorate. We took a break and considered the next move.

Deciding on a new approach line, we cleared away the forward door of the compartment and were able to get to the base of the bomb to view the fuse. This one was definitely armed as the screw-piece was missing and all safety devices were thus removed.

By now we were working very well together and had become quite used to the presence of the weapon, so that the lads now named it 'Big Bad Bomb'. At this stage the MEO of *Fearless* arrived with his team of Stokers offering 'help'. Although this interruption did give us a welcome break, it was not at all convenient and I sent him off with Piggy to 'look at' the *Lancelot* bomb.

Soon enough we had most of the debris cleared away and could start to think about moving the Beast. First though, it must be slung. Using a helicopter strop, some steel wire rope, shackles, bulldog grips and lashing rope, we soon had the BBB trussed up and ready to lift off the sprung bulkhead which it had squashed.

Using a pair of chain tackles, which we pulled through a link at a time on the control side, we gradually took up the weight. We had managed to remove the alloy sheet in which it had partially wrapped itself, but only after some difficulty and a back-wrenching injury to myself, the sort from which one never properly recovers.

After a long time, operating the tackles as slowly as we were able, keeping the chains from touching anything else, and all the while operating steadying lines, we had the weapon suspended free of all obstructions. This had been done so carefully that Big Bad Bomb was still quite convinced that it had not moved at all.

There was a convenient series of hatches above the inboard after corner of the compartment and a handy crane above that. Having opened these up and located a willing crane driver, we were set to start moving the bomb out of the ship. Everyone not involved was now put into a couple of the lifeboats which were streamed off the stern. There they would be safe if our plan did not work.

The crane hook was lowered to just inside the hatch, and we set about moving the 'nasty' across to it. We had to be careful to keep the endless chains of the tackles away from it, or else a vibration could be set up with untoward results. As slowly as we had moved it before, the Beast was slung over to the hatchway and attached to the crane hook.

'Hoist away!'

The hook lowered.

'Stop!'

The hook stopped.

'It's going the wrong way. It's lowering instead of hoisting.'

'OK.'

'Hoist away!'

The hook lowered.

'Stop!'

The hook stopped.

'It's doing it again.'

We only had one more chance. If the crane lowered again it was likely to drop the bomb on the deck.

'Hoist away!'

The hook started to rise slowly.

Using steadying lines to keep the bomb diagonally across the hatchway, the only way it would fit through, we managed to raise it through two decks and out over the side. Lowering carefully, we directed it into the rubber boat in which we had made a nest of cornflakes boxes which, with the help of a couple of Board of Trade lifejackets, held it in the exact position we wanted.

Tommo and Buster took the ship's Gemini, in which crouched the BBB, in tow behind our own and got it well clear of the ship's side. Here they slashed all the buoyancy tanks to allow the whole lot to sink to the bottom. This it refused to do. Not knowing where the other ships were, but being aware that they were drifting in the freshening wind, Tommo considered that they might soon be blown down on to one of the darkened hulls, with possible devastating results. Time for immediate action. As carefully as they could in the dark, with only a couple of helmet torches to light their way, they eased the bomb over the side of the waterlogged Gemini and let it sink to the bottom. A most courageous and selfless act.

The operation over, we reeled in the men in the lifeboats and had a party in the Wardroom – for it was great to be alive.

None of the Team were happy with the air raid situation. After all, here were the flower of the Royal Navy, men highly trained and motivated, possessed of that extra spark so vital to the Clearance Diver, and they were required to lie on the deck of their mess in a great pile of bodies and to put their hands over their heads. Not the sort of behaviour that the boys naturally took to and they communicated this openly and in short order.

A reappraisal of the Team's resources indicated that, should we lose our Gemini-boats, we would be in shtuck. Thus it was decreed that, when an air raid was signalled, those nearest to the boats would take them ashore, out of the line of fire as it were.

Air Raid Warning Red! and two Geminis of happy, smiling Divers headed for the shore and a grandstand view of the proceedings. Or perhaps not so grand, for as the defence hotted up, more and more spent and stray ammunition found its way into our vicinity, so that before long the happy, smiling Divers were dodging their own side's bullets. (It is a wonder that the helos survived for they were hovering close by.) Plan B therefore: next time an alert is given, take the Geminis to bow and to stern, look to see where the attack is coming from, and dodge round the other side. In this way we kept our boats whole and the lads interested.

Later, when diving on the *Antelope* and having no radios to give notice of incoming attacks, one man would watch the helos at all times. Should they all suddenly make for the shore and hover among the hillocks, then get the diver up quickly and head for shelter. However, it takes time to surface a diver, so for the moment there they had to remain, in the Gemini, dressed in their bright red cold-water diving suits, anxiously watching the skies and hills.

Imagine yourself to be an Argentinian pilot swooping low over San Carlos Water, weaving and twisting at high speed, hoping that no one will lock on to you with a Rapier. There are many ships to be seen, but in the middle is a great space of empty water (*Antelope* danger area), in the centre of which there appears to be a large, bright red 'thing'. Where would you jettison your bomb?

The boys moved from *Bedivere* to Red Beach by LCT, stopping on the way at various ships. Alongside one, a lanky dark-haired individual of the Press decided that the Team was a fitting subject for study and, pointing a camera in their direction, commenced shooting off film. The lads were not particularly impressed by this and informed the individual accordingly. He retired in short order, probably to plot revenge. We were later informed that this was the now-famous Max Hastings, but we never saw him again.

Arriving at Red Beach, FCDT 3 were given the seaward corner of the old refrigeration station as their 'site'. Positioning the chacons to form a three-sided box, and removing four of the six doors to make a roof, they arrived at a three room house with courtyard, fully weatherproof (sort of), in which to set up the necessary 'clean area' needed for diving workshop and store. Other boxes and cases were piled into walls and some crated outboard engines of the RM variety were found, creating a relatively shrapnel-proof construction. This was named Fort Thompson after its instigator – Tommo.

Within the compound was pitched a borrowed tent, named Rose Cottage, where other stores were kept. Later duck-boards were procured to combat the mud problem. From this excellent piece of improvisation operations were conducted for the next 18 days.

Hot water, of which there was very little, was limited to the hospital, but some was allowed us for washing off breathing sets, which must perforce be kept ultra-hygienic. If there was any spare, it was doled out by the pint for personal hygiene, and we all became adept at having a good 'bird bath' in such a small quantity.

MEDIA GAMES

>Now is the battle-roar of tanks
>Seen to splash through shallows in the sands.
>Now is the smell of victory
>Tangent from a box within your hands.
>Now is the pilot viewed, loosing
>Smarter weapons into foreign lands.
>Now is the soldier's spousal tear
>Watched in close-up as the news demands.
>Now is triumph squeezed (Take seven!)
>From the fighter, warlike as he stands.
>Now is used the replay function,
>Haunting TV's colour channel bands.

(Although this poem was written in 1991 during the much-vaunted Gulf War against Iraq, I consider that it has a place here since it represents the thinking of servicemen at such times.)

A short stop in *Intrepid*, to have a hole in Ginge's LCT fixed, allowed a welcome, if enforced, break and the chance for an hour's sleep. This was rudely interrupted by an air raid, and up came the dock door at the stern of the ship. There we were amongst the baggage awaiting the outcome. With nothing else to do but sit there, perhaps a little fiddle playing would be in order. Well, if you've got to go, what better way? It certainly takes your mind off things. Suddenly there came the 'voice of God' from the Dock Control position broadcast speaker, 'TURN THAT

BLOODY RADIO OFF . . . !!!! Oh, sorry Bernie – carry on, mate.'

25.5.82 Thursday
Up at 0830 and off to *Sir L* to shore up the bomb. At first light 3 LCTs started to move the ship under the direction of the Chief Officer [Chief Officer of RFA *Sir Lancelot*, Second in Command; affectionately known as the 'Choff'] and an RCT [Royal Corps of Transport] Major. Very windy but at present moving OK. Lads rabbiting gear [collecting stores needed for the task]. Piggy, Rex and I on the bridge – picnicking.

It had been decided to move *Lancelot* away from the other ships and out of any projected bombing path. Thus, in the early morning and in a rising wind, Piggy's team went on board. The first priority was to shore the UXB so that it would not fall over and detonate during the move.

We approached the ship from astern, in true Divers' fashion, and climbed the wire ladders we had left hanging before. But something was wrong; things had changed and the galley was in a shambles. A search revealed that, while we had been engaged in other things, another bomb from one of the previous day's air raids had struck her port side, gouged a long groove in the upper works and deflected over the side into the sea. The damage within was extensive, but at least we still had only the one uninvited guest to deal with.

Piggy and I examined the brute and decided upon the best way to shore it. This we proceeded to do ever so carefully. There is a certain delicacy required when knocking in wedges next to one of these things. However, by use of these and some breast-shoring we achieved our end and retired to the bridge for the move. Meanwhile the rest of the team, except for Rex who came with us as messenger, searched the ship for the gear we would need for what looked like being a protracted removal. On the bridge, the three of us had a picnic while the Chief Officer, a man of piratical aspect, and an RCT Major directed the three LCTs as tugs. In such a situation the taste of compo turkey-paste on 'biscuits A/B' becomes exotic and memorable in the extreme. We looked down from the height of the bridge to watch the LCTs, on long tow-lines, butting into the foam-streaked sea which, even in the shelter of the inlet, resembled classic storm conditions.

Slowly, seeming almost not to be moving, the injured and abused vessel was dragged to her destined anchorage; but LCTs are not tugs and ships with unexploded bombs on board are not nice things to shunt around in a gale. Although she was not perhaps exactly in her designated spot, eventually the anchor bit home and she came to her cable, in rather less water than we would have wished but safe enough.

Anchored the Ship rather near the shore in a strong wind which made handling difficult. Got a lift back to Red Beach with LCT and spent the rest of the afternoon sorting out gear on a wee corner of real estate we have been given. Gave Teapot my hammock, for which he was grateful and also a bottle of chili sauce from Fiddler. Still meeting lots of people. Reaction to Bomb Team is good, especially by the medics.

1935. AIR ATTACK IN PROGRESS. 2 × A/C overflew low and 2 rockets exploded, one 20ft to the left and another behind the Chacon to the right. 1943. Several explosions on the foreshore.

After the raid, which took out the cookhouse, we found 2 × UXB. One on the shore. One on the heights to the north plus one tail section, so looking for another.

Later. There were 8 × 500lb bombs. '1' exploded outside the galley injuring 20 and killing 3, one more died later. '2' went into the refrigerating machinery in the mess back of the galley and '3' landed on the deckhead there. '4' exploded in the sea. '5' did not but lay on the low water mark. '6' was discovered atop the hill and later high-ordered by the RAF EOD. One other

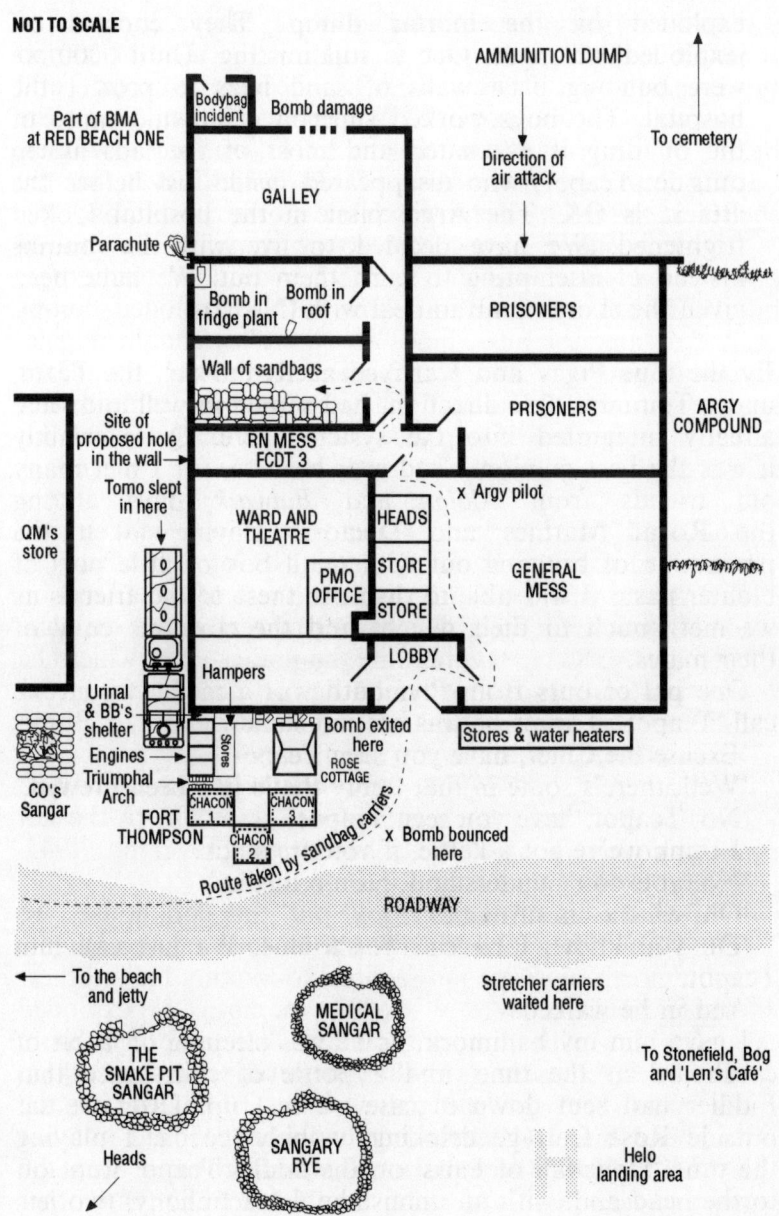

exploded by the mortar dump. They cooked off [exploded] all night. One is still missing. Until 0300 we were building blast walls of sand bags to protect the hospital. The boys worked superbly. Half and more of the building is evacuated and most of the lads asleep outside. Teapot, who disappeared inside just before the attack, is OK. The Argie pilot in the hospital looked frightened. We have decided to live with the bombs instead of attempting to burn them out. We have been given the shore bomb to deal with (No. 5).

By the time Piggy and I arrived at Red Beach the Team, under Tommo's able direction, had settled in well and were already integrated into the system there. Quite frankly it was the best reunion I had ever been to, for I met many old friends from *Albion* and *Bulwark* days among the Royal Marines and Doctors. Having taken the precaution of bringing out with me a box of little pots of bloater paste, I was able to dispense these to old friends as we met, much to their delight and the covetous envy of their mates.

One pal of ours from Plymouth was a medic whom we call 'Teapot'. I knew he was around somewhere.

'Excuse me Chief, have you seen Teapot?'

'Well, there's some in that fanny that's just been brewed.'

'No, Teapot, have you seen Teapot?'

'I think we've got a kettle, if you are stuck.'

'No, you don't understand. He's a medic.'

'Oh, what's his surname?'

'Do you know, I haven't got a clue. We just call him Teapot.'

And in he walked.

I gave him my hammock, as he was sleeping on a bit of cardboard at the time, and a bottle of chili sauce that Fiddler had sent down in case we met up. Later we sat outside Rose Cottage drinking 'wobbly' cocoa, I playing the tune 'Downfall of Paris' on the fiddle. Teapot went off to the head and, with an unmistakable cacophony, two jets passed low over the hospital in the gloaming. Then the bombs started exploding.

A Royal Marine Senior, caught in the open, dashed into Fort Thompson and sought refuge in the chacon in front of me. He looked a little surprised to see a bearded Naval Lieutenant counting the explosions as they occurred and writing it all down in a notebook – but what else was there to do? Soon enough, however, people were out and about and the search for UXBs was joined. It is at times like this that really strange things happen, such as: two bomb disposal officers (one RN, one RAF) converging from a distance on the same bomb, at the run, shouting at each other, 'It's mine!'

'No, it's not. It's mine!'

'It can't be. It's below the high-water mark!'

'No, it's above it!'

It turned out to be below the high-water mark and the Navy won the prize – the prize!

The upshot of all this activity was that two bombs were found in the hospital and various others at later stages. One had passed through the roof, smashed through the front gable-end, bounced in the 'road' a few feet away from the boss surgeon, Commander Rick Jolly, and flown up on to the ridge above the bog. Later we found a long sliver of tail section and presented it to this bear-like officer as a trophy. He thanked us and said he would mount it as a modern sculpture called 'Adrenalin is Brown'.

There was a meeting of senior people to decide what to do. Should the hospital be evacuated or what? Alan Swan, our resident bomb expert, counselled that we should live with the bombs where they were, but as they were likely fitted with time delays should quickly build sandbag blast-walls to protect the hospital, evacuating certain areas only. FCDT 3 took on the responsibility of building the walls.

For six-and-a-half hours we filled and carried sandbags topped up with wet gravel from the beach. From each bag a dribble of freezing black mud would saturate our shoulders and run down the back of our necks. It was boring and monotonous work, but vital to the safety of all.

Trudge, trudge; carry, carry; slosh, slosh; mutter, mutter: the endless line of mud-blackened men moved to and fro through the doors and passages, down to the beach and back. Mutter, mutter; slosh, slosh; trudge, trudge.

There was an Argy pilot who had been shot down a day or so before and picked up by Ginge in his LCT. (This was about the time that it had been hit by one of our own Sea Cat missiles, luckily dud, causing the hole that had delayed us in Intrepid.) This pilot was lying on a camp-bed, nursing a broken arm, just by one of the doorways frequented by the trudging stream of filthy, wild-eyed men carrying sandbags. Being one of the first Argies we had seen, he was something of a curiosity and viewed as such by each passing man. Trudge, trudge; carry, carry; mutter, mutter; look at Argy. The poor fellow must have been convinced that he was about to become part of the wall at any minute. The blast wall was completed, under the leadership of Charlie Smithard, Phil and Tommo, at three in the morning. Using their inspired constructional techniques, it was sufficiently reinforced to take the bullet-like force of the fuse should a detonation occur. A room had been left clear between it and the hospital ward to act as a void and catchment area for debris. For this first night everyone was evacuated from the danger area and crowded into the remaining space. Next day the Team claimed the cleared room as their living area, and set up their hammocks and camp-beds accordingly, thus transforming it into a regular 'ship's mess-deck'.

We had finished building, casualties had been tended and things had returned again to normal, when I met up with Teapot. Having last seen him disappearing into the building just before the enemy struck, I had not expected to see him again. Consequently it was with relief and joy that I heard his voice behind me saying, 'Bernie, don't you EVER play "Downfall of Paris" in daylight again!'

We were lucky that time. Half the Team was in the Galley, eating, when the RM Corporal Chef in charge told them, 'Come on you Divers; go eat your scran somewhere else.'

'OK Lenny', and out they trooped through one of the heavy doors and into the building. As the door shut the attack came in. A few moments earlier and our numbers would have been severely reduced.

Lenny survived, and moved his galley away across to the other side of the valley. Only allowed food at dawn and dusk, we had to cross a stone-field and a bog to get there.

HOSPITAL BLAST-WALL

Softly now and mind your noise.
Don't disturb the wounded boys
Sleeping.

Though they dribble down your neck,
Put the sandbags on the deck,
Weeping.

Use the shingle from the shore.
Bring a couple hundred more,
Dripping.

Roundly! With a turn – belay!
Detonator's on delay,
Slipping.

Time is short, so lift and haul;
Got to thicken up this wall,
Stacking.

'Beat the clock to beat the bomb!'
Such a fitting axiom -
Cracking!

Strip to trousers, boots and belt.
Push yourself until you melt
Sweating.

> Heave 'em up; no time to lose,
> Only minutes on the fuse
> Setting.
>
> Hacked it, with a bag to spare!
> Finest bulwark anywhere -
> Lasting.
>
> Let the sucker detonate;
> No way it can penetrate
> Blasting.

28.5.82 Friday
Up at 0930 with message to get over to *Intrepid* for 'brief'. Once there managed a hot shower, dhobi [naval expression for washing one's clothes] and a sandwich. Then on to *Lancelot* (via home) to work through the day on the bomb [RFA *Sir Lancelot*]. Wrote a report on the *Galahad* job [when not involved with helping Piggy].

The job took 22 hours altogether. Hairy moments: when I picked debris out of the pistol [fuse] with a dental tooth pick; when the sheerlegs [a bipod or gin used for lifting heavy weights, made out of handy lengths of timber and cordage] started to slip and the bomb to fall; when the chain sling slipped; when lowering the bomb to the water and it nudged the accommodation ladder.

The lads were good and Piggy did well. I did the slinging and the shoring. The Chief Chippy [Chief Petty Officer Shipwright Siddle] cut away one cabin and a staircase above the bomb. Finished 1000 on 29th.

The first thing to do, after the films had been removed from around the bomb, was to find out if the thing was armed. It was only possible to get at the fuse by leaning right over the casing and resting one's head on the debris on the far side. At least there was no acid around this time. In this position, working upside down, the fuse could

ELEVATION

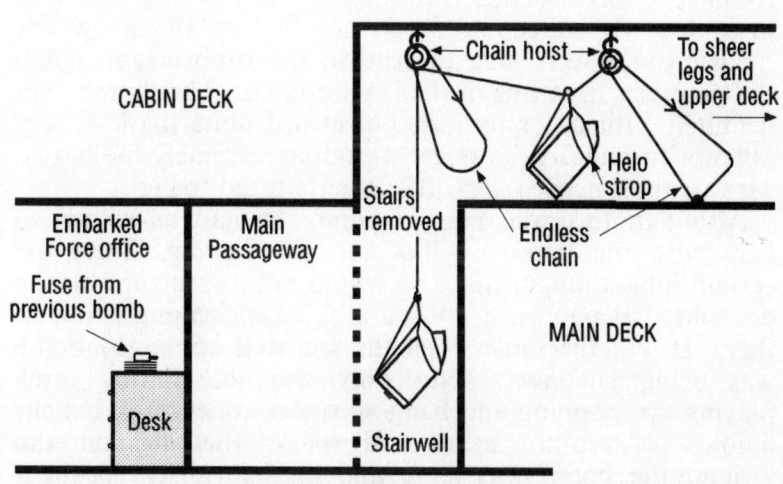

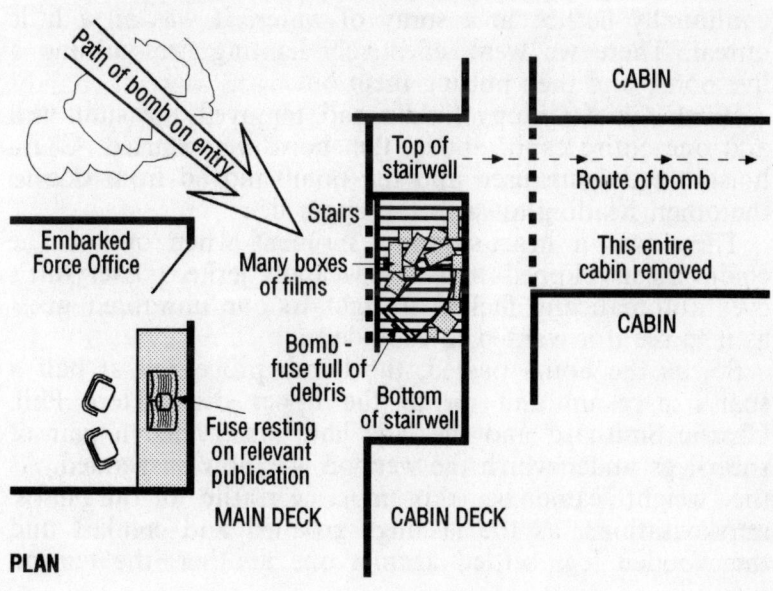

PLAN

be cleared. The safety screw was still in place and the spaces around it were filled with packed asbestos and formica. Using a dentist's toothpick and working delicately in a clockwise direction, so as not to turn the screw any further out, I was able to remove the rubbish and count the number of turns it had unscrewed. The bomb was definitely armed – only just, but armed none the less. Any attempt to reinsert the screw would be extremely foolhardy. This weapon needed very little excuse to go 'bang'.

Although this was Piggy's bomb, he had asked me to help with the graunchy bits and the rigging. There are certain jobs, though, that you would not ask anyone else to do, jobs that you must do yourself. Fuse cleaning is one of them. It was the same when the stairwell above the bomb was being cut away. Not only was the cutting torch playing up, popping and banging (most unnerving), but the amount of red-hot metal and sparks that fell on and around the bomb was large and constant. Here again it was Piggy and I doing the flame-dousing. We had the thing covered in woollen blankets and an asbestos curtain and continually bathed in a spray of water. It was all a little unreal. There we were, effectively lighting fires around a live bomb and then putting them out.

When Chief Chippy Siddle had removed the stair well and one entire cabin above, the 'hoist' was started. Chain hoists were again used and the bomb moved from one to the other, heading towards the upper deck.

There was a heart-stopping moment when one of the chain hoists slipped and the weapon jerked. Everyone's eyes automatically flicked straight to our unwanted guest as if to see if it wanted to explode.

So, as the hours passed, the bomb proceeded at half a snail's pace up and on to the upper deck. Here Phil, Charlie Smithard and the lads had constructed a pair of sheer-legs under which the weapon was now suspended. As the weight came on this most versatile of all naval improvisations, as the lashings groaned and creaked and the wooden legs settled against one another, the tension

HMS JUNELLA- When this photograph was taken, from RFA *Sir Bedivere* off Ascension Island, we had little idea how close our links were to become. We were just glad not to be going into the Southern Ocean '. . . in that!'

SURVIVAL SUIT PARTY - Left to right: Phil, Tommo, Dave, Wheels, Buster, Jock I, Joe, Charlie, John Boy, Jock II, Rex. Note one of the 1942 Bofors guns in the background.

FRIGHTENING FIFTIES – *Sir Bedivere* plowing into the teeth of a force 8. (Note: second row of containers from left, third container from aft – box on top is our Detonator Tank.)

BB AND 'THE BIG BAD BOMB' – The 1000lb bomb, wrapped in a wasted sheet of metal, lies amongst the acid-soaked debris of the battery charging room – hence the 'No Smoking' sign.

BUSTER AND WHISKEY put the final touches to the sling around the bomb. From this angle the problem of removing the alloy sheet without disturbing the weapon can be fully appreciated.

'ALL CLEAR' John Lawyer's painting depicts in startling detail the tense moment of getting the bomb away from the ship's side. Buster in the bow and Tommo driving the engine are watched anxiously by Whiskey and BB in the bows of the *Sir Galahad*.

RED BEACH ONE – Centre: the hospital building with Fort Thompson at its left end eaves about a third of the way along from the left end. Lenny's cafe is at the bottom is unloading at the beach.

FORT THOMPSON AND ROSE COTTAGE – Not a lot of space but enough. The corner of the building, behind the sandbags, was the urinal-head and BB's chosen air raid shelter. To the left is one of the two entrances, known as the Triumphal Arch.

front. The exit hole from one of the bombs that hit it can be seen just under the right and Rick Willer's trench at bottom left. Colour-Sergeant 'Ginge's landing craft

GEORGE SIDDLE AND THE *LANCELOT* BOMB – Note the shores and wedges holding the bomb steady, also the lack of space around it.

'HANDSOMELY' (Navalese for gently) – Again artist John Lawyer has expertly recreated the scene as the bomb is lowered from the RFA *Sir Lancelot*. The gash made by the second bomb can be seen just astern of the lifeboat, and on the starboard quarter is the rope-ladder we used for boarding.

THE 'MESS-DECK' – Chas Smithard is on the right with camera in hand, and Phil on the left; BB in the white sweater. Note the hammocks slung from the meat-hook rails.

PHIL AND CHAS writing letters home.

THE *ANTELOPE* DECK PLATE – Piggy and BB with the deck plate from *Antelope*'s gangway. (Photo taken in FCDT 3 'mess-deck'.)

SURGEON COMMANDER RICK 'THE BEAR' JOLLY – i/c The Red and Green Life Machine.

WINCHING THE BOYS ONTO *TRISTRAM'S* DECK.

was almost tangible. Eventually the transfer was complete and we were ready for the next, equally hazardous phase.

The bipod was swayed gently outboard and the weapon, now connected to a lengthy and hefty piece of rope, was about to be lowered to the sea bed. Guide-lines were taken to the upper deck fore and aft and to Geminis off the ship's side, the rope was paid out and the bomb lowered. There was a certain amount of consternation when it nudged the accommodation ladder, but then it was below the surface and on its way deep into the mud on the bottom. Once the rope went slack, we knew it was there, cut the hawser and allowed the end to fall into the sea. The weapon was still somewhere under the ship but we hoped that there was enough water and deep enough mud, even in this removed anchorage, to protect the *Lancelot* from too much damage if there was an explosion.

This had been the long one. From start to finish it had taken twenty-two hours and a lot of that time had been in daylight. Luckily no air raids had affected us and hopefully we would get no more jobs like that one.

29.5.82 *Saturday*

1536. An Argy jet's just been zapped by a Rapier. Took ages to get back from *Intrepid* but did eventually and went for to crash-out. However, such a lovely day that I took fiddle for a walk instead – until the above.

Mike Crabtree, an old Shipmate in *Bulwark*, pilot, visited and with self and Rick Jolly had a look at our tame bomb.

We've heard that Darwin is surrounded and the 'As' have taken civilian hostages. Lots of casualties coming now and 'A' prisoners.

The wounded arrived in large and small numbers at the hospital. All we ever knew, and could watch for, was that a helo burning landing lights (bright spotlights shining ahead) and coming in at a rate of knots had casualties aboard. Then whatever was on hand took second place until the wounded were safely in hospital. On such occasions, even though an air raid 'red' should sound, there was always a queue of men on the 'road' waiting to rush toward the next helo to land on the valley floor.

When the Team were not working on other things, they would always keep themselves handy for stretcher parties or anything else required by the medics. Often they would be found in the hospital observing operations and wounds being tended. They were convinced that there would come a day when they would be needed in there, and were determined to ensure that they would be used to the sight of all the blood and gore when that day arrived. How right they proved to be.

> Crashed out about 2300. Teapot came round for a jar/tot and a tune. Sleeping in a tent, inside Fort Thompson, called Rose Cottage. Very cold during the night and it snowed.

> *30.5.82 Sunday*
> Spent the morning (afternoon) on board *Sir Lancelot* having a bath and dhobi. Needed that and felt much better afterwards. In the evening was ordered across to *Fearless* to meet the press. Took Tommo and we were filmed for TV about the two bombs. Played it straight down the middle – no bullshit. They seemed rapt. Afterwards caught a quick glimpse of the video and didn't we look mean!

I was half-way down a Jacob's ladder on *Lancelot*'s port side, about to get into a Gemini with my ever-present winger Tommo, when the Engineer Commander from *Fearless* hailed me.

'The press want to interview you.'

I suggested that they might find better people to do that to, but he replied quite clearly, 'No, you don't understand. You ARE to be interviewed by the press.'

'Aye-aye, sir.'

So off went Tommo and I in our rubber boat to whichever ship it was, *Fearless* or *Intrepid* – we could never tell. Actually it did not really matter, because our 'tasker' Lieutenant Commander Meatyard always contrived to be on board to welcome us. We were directed toward the chapel, the inner sanctum given over to the television people. They were very nice to us, sat us down, gave us an enormous steak supper, a bottle of wine, coffee and a large lump of whisky. By the time we had consumed that lot and got used to the warmth of the ship, we were not feeling like moving anyway and were quite ready for the interview.

Having seen the way some interviewees are treated on television, I was determined to do this one right. The Navy wanted me to tell the story: OK, I would tell it; not just answer questions. Tommo did the same and, looking magnificently piratical, came over great.

Brian Hanrahan and Mike Nicholson were doing the biz and I think my mate Jeremy Hands was there also. No matter – they looked after us well, got what they wanted and gave me a copy of the tape later (which was unfortunately stolen by a burglar). The only stipulation we made, and made clearly, was that they should not use the material for broadcast until after the war was over. As we pointed out, some misguided soul had been saying on UK television that the bombs were being dropped too low and were not exploding. The next thing would be that the enemy would drop UXBs on purpose, specially rigged to take out the Bomb Disposal men: that meant me, and I was not particularly keen on the prospect. I do not believe that it was malicious: the media just do not think of these things in their scramble to get a good story. Anyway, after this conversation, not another mention of the matter was made in a broadcast.

Here is the gist of what was said:

30.5.82
'NEWS AT TEN' INTERVIEW SHOWN JULY 1982: LT BERNIE BRUEN RN, FALKLANDS BOMB SQUAD.

Introduction by Alastair Burnet:

'One of the Royal Navy bomb disposal men in the Falklands fighting has been talking quietly about his job there. Lieutenant Bernie Bruen had to deal with two 1,000-pound Argentine bombs that hit *Sir Galahad* but didn't explode. That was before the Bluff Cove attack, when 50 men died in *Sir Galahad*. Only 24 hours earlier, one of Lieutenant Bruen's colleagues died while trying to defuse a similar bomb in HMS *Antelope*.

BB: The bomb in Sir Galahad entered on the port side, on the shade deck, smashed through about three compartments and, picking up bits as it went, eventually ended up in the battery charging room. As I say, it collected a lot of debris, and one of the bits of debris it collected was a large sheet of alloy which was folded in two and wrapped neatly round the bomb, which therefore made it a lot bigger object than it would have been otherwise. It also smashed through a lot of batteries and carboys and sprayed the whole place with acid, so the clearance of the debris was not very pleasant. As you can see, we got our clothes and things burned with it. We had to keep washing our hands off every few minutes in a bucket of water. We did the initial reconnoitre of it and tried to discover exactly what it was and whether it was live or not. We considered that it was. Then I came down to clear it with my team, Leading Seaman Thompson, Able Seaman Mottram and Able Seaman Walker.

The first thing to do was to get all the debris out of the way. Leading Seaman Thompson took charge of that with the two lads, and did a very good job clearing away all the loose stuff, a lot of rubbish, heavy stuff and light. You had to do this very quietly of course to stop any vibrations .... possibly to the bomb .... set it off.

... anyway they did an extremely good job, even so far as to sweeping the floor and getting it nice and clean so that we wouldn't slip and knock things. To start off with, of course, there was a lot of gymnastics to get over the debris; hanging from the deckhead to try and get to places so you could pass things out. Having done that, we decided on the route we were going to use and how we were going to take it out. We thought the best thing to do was to lift it, remove this large piece of metal that was round it, take it underneath the hatch, up two decks and then crane it over the side ...

.... so we set that up.

We then had a coffee break, a little bit of music, before we started. The rest of the ship's company, the engineers and everybody, went and sat in a lifeboat streamed off astern, so they were quite safe. We started off.

Normally on these occasions you would try to do it remotely. The first move anyway you do remotely, with long leads, and a very long way away. It was not possible in this case for various reasons. One, because the actual lead we got from our blocks was slightly forward of directly above the bomb. There was this large piece of metal all around it. Also, underneath was a piece of metal which was under stress, which could move it. So in fact, all in all, we had to manhandle it, all four of us there, and it was a question of the man on the outboard side operating his tackle and keeping the chains away from this metal bit as well, so it wouldn't vibrate, and also standing on the metal which was under stress to try and keep that down.

Tommo here, on the inboard side, was doing the same thing and also prising the metal apart on his side, Whiskey Walker at the front, with his rope, was trying to pull the bomb like a sort of pendulum, pull it forward, whilst I sat underneath it supporting the bomb on my knees and lifting it off. This took about twenty minutes to achieve because we had to do a lot of jiggling around one way or another, but we eventually managed to get it off and the bomb underneath the crane.

The crane driver then came along, and we hooked up and started to lift. Unfortunately the crane wasn't working too well at that time, and when we tried to lift it . . . . it lowered . . . . and lots of cries of 'stop!' After several attempts, we managed to get it to go upwards, but it didn't leave us very much room underneath . . . . getting closer and closer to the deck . . . but we got it up.

Now at this stage there was a nasty squall blowing, and the wind was getting up and putting a bit of movement on the bomb, so we had to have four steadying lines. A thousand pounds is a lot to steady when you've got maybe . . . forty feet of crane wire . . . . so that was fairly . . . fairly graunchy I think, because we had to go through a hatch which didn't leave us much room . . . . We had to take it diagonally across the hatch to get it out; then we got it to the top, swung it overboard, and lowered it into a Gemini full of cornflakes packets, which I thought was the best thing really to absorb any shock from the waves and to let it nestle in, so that it wouldn't move. Then Leading Seaman Thompson took the Gemini away under tow with Able Seaman Mottram. The idea was to let the air out of the Gemini and sink the Gemini with the bomb in it. This unfortunately didn't work, so they slashed the Gemini tanks, and still it wouldn't sink. And so, with great presence of mind, and very, very carefully, they both got into the sinking Gemini and eased the bomb over the side.

. . . and that was the clearance.

Interviewer: You were convinced while you were working on the bomb that it was primed, it was ready to go off, there was a fuse in it.

BB: Oh yes, yes.

Interviewer: You had to keep it at a certain angle, I presume.

BB: Right. The problem about these particular fuses is that any way you knock it will let the fuse off. Any way and it will go, and these bombs sometimes come in sideways. So one of the problems is that if you tilt it so that the nose is down, if there is something loose inside it, it could strike against the detonator, or could move it some way. So we had to keep the bomb just slightly nose up . . . . we didn't have it very much nose up, but it was just slightly nose up.

Interviewer: How long did all this take?

BB: That clearance took eight-and-a-half hours.

Interviewer: Have you had to deal with anything like this before?

BB: No. This is the first time. I've been in the Branch for some time, but I've been away doing other things. This is the first actual live

	one I've done.
Interviewer:	So how did you know what to do? Did you get the instruction book and go through it?
BB:	No. We get trained in it. Our job is clearance of underwater mines, mostly Second World War stuff and any sort of ordnance that the Navy might use .... like it might be a smoke candle or something like that. Most of the stuff is last world war mines and of course bombs .... I mean, if a bomb fell in the sea or something like that .... so proprietary ordnance you might say ....
Interviewer:	Now the second bomb you went for, I gather you did a little bit of dentistry work on it.
BB:	Yes .... in fact the second bomb was not my bomb. The second bomb was Chief Petty Officer Trotter's. He's my number two in the team.
Interviewer:	You didn't fight over it, did you?
BB:	No .... No ... in fact we have a distinct rule, you see. Everybody has a go at one bomb if there are enough to go round, and you try not to make people have to go at two bombs ... you know ... if possible, because obviously you want to minimise the risk. So in fact it was Chief Trotter's bomb, and he worked out the whole thing. I went along really to give him a hand and do the close-in work with him. When you start messing around with pistols ... that is what we call the fuse on the end of a bomb ... everyone else goes away. And it was in order to find out whether it was armed or not that we had to remove a lot of debris that was inside, virtually standing on our heads at the same time, because there was very little room, you know, sort of coming over the top, without touching the bomb ... get your head

	down . . . squeeze in . . . and we removed the gash in the fuse with a dentist's pick, which we found was the best thing to scrape little bits away at a time, just enough to show us what we wanted to see, and then . . . we knew . . . that it was live.
Interviewer:	Was this a difficult one to deal with? This one took you a lot longer, didn't it?
BB:	This one took us twenty-two hours.
Interviewer:	Non-stop?
BB:	Non-stop, yes.
Intervierer:	Don't you start to get . . . you know . . . physically shaky? You obviously have no nerves, but I mean your muscles must start to shake after all that time.
BB:	No, you don't actually. I would have agreed with you beforehand, I would have thought so, but it's not true. You are so involved in what you are doing that, as far as you are concerned, it is really just an article that has to be removed without breaking it. It almost sounds blasé to say that, but that is it. I think you come to terms very quickly with the fact that you are dealing with a large amount of explosives. For example, we don't wear body armour . . . what's the point?
Interviewer:	But twenty-two-and-a-half hours . . . All right, so your muscles and your mind kept going, but didn't you find there were distractions, that you started to wander . . . because it's a helluva long time to be working at such a thing at such close range. Could you manage to concentrate yourself?
BB:	Well, you've got to appreciate that most of that, or a lot of that twenty-two hours is in fact physical work of rigging, cutting stuff away, removing gash, thinking about what you are going to do next, a lot of the time in

close proximity to the bomb, obviously because that is where you are working. I think if you were going to do twenty-two hours of actually sort of nipping things away inside, yes, I think you're probably right. But on this particular occasion, it's there, and it hasn't gone off, and as long as you don't move it, it won't. It's only when you start moving it and start playing with it that you perhaps, maybe start thinking about it, but by that stage, you have got so used to the fact that it's there that you just crack on and do it.

Interviewer: You've got to live with it.
BB: Yes.
Interviewer: Do you do very much with it or do you isolate it and take it away? Do you have to try and fiddle with bits inside it?
BB: No. They did try that earlier on, as you know, and it was decided not to do that. Once you get a fuse in that condition, once it's armed itself, basically it's saying, 'I want to stay here, I don't want to come out.' Now you can, indeed, yes you can take it out. There are ways of doing it, but we're talking about this particular situation and in this particular situation, with the fuse we had, and the condition they were in ... they'd been bashed about a bit ... that fuse was saying to me very loud and clear, 'I want to stay here, I don't want to come out.'
Interviewer: So you calculate the risks, and it's safer to try and move the whole bomb, live as it is, than to try to defuse it on the spot?
BB: Apart from anything else, we had very little room to try and fit equipment to remove it. But there are all sorts of ways we could have done it. We could have bored into it and

	removed the explosives, or burned it out, or what have you, but with the various parameters that were on us, with the time we had, the situation with the bomb, where it was, and what equipment we'd got available, etcetera, etcetera, we decided that the easiest and the best way was to lift it.
Interviewer:	I gather, Bernie, that you played the violin afterwards.
BB:	Yeah! Well, it's a good way of relaxing.
Interviewer:	Why do you play the violin every time you defuse a bomb?
BB:	I think it is sheer relief, and joy to be alive, I don't know. I enjoy playing my fiddle and the lads like listening to it as well . . . well, they haven't told me they don't yet.
Interviewer:	I gather also that you recited a poem, can you tell me what it was?
BB:	Oh yes, it was a poem called 'The Impossible Task', which is just a little spoof poem which I wrote. It's a kind of 'Think-of-England' type poem with a surprise ending.
Interviewer:	Can you do it?
BB:	What, now?
Interviewer:	Yes . . . tell us?
BB:	Well, I wonder if I can remember it. Yes, you have to . . . we really should have a Union Jack behind us to do this but . . . (Bernie recites 'The Impossible Task'.) As I say, it's a silly little poem . . .
Interviewer:	I don't think there's much more to say after that, Bernie . . . great stuff . . . congratulations. Thank you.

Back ashore after a steak supper (mmm!) and after a party at Rose Cottage, Piggy had been given a bottle of St Emilion by Mike Nicholson as his appreciation for what he'd done. Nice touch! Got a job removing life-raft from an LCU [Landing Craft (Unspecified)]. Eventually got to bed at 0100. Another cold night.

THE IMPOSSIBLE TASK

(an original composition normally delivered in Shakespearian tones of the most pompous kind)

They said that it could not be done.
They said it was impossible.
They said no man, however strong,
Could do what was not possible.
They said that many men had tried,
In every way they knew,
And though they'd tried, they all had failed,
This thing so hard to do.
He said that he did not believe it was so very hard.
He said that he would strive and
Then this thing he would retard;
For was there not a tiny seed in every English heart
That, nurtured with the will to win,
Could form a greater part
And grow with care, like English oak,
Its roots grow deeper yet,
Its branches spread and leaves extend,
Until the task was met?
And should this seed of courage grow,
Along with gross endeavour,
It should eclipse the baser tasks,
Till they are gone forever.
For man, no matter where he is, no matter who he be,
Can overcome and rise again and do the greatest deeds;
And when he's strived and gained that part
Where heroes always stood,
He'll count himself with greater men,
And join their brotherhood.
And so he said that he would try

This thing to overcome,
And strive with all his might and main
Until his task was done.
They said that it could not be done,
They said that he would rue it,
But he faced the challenge and he found -
He couldn't bloody do it!

BB

(alternative ending for those of a more serious nature:
'. . . . and he found – that only He could do it.')

Rose Cottage
Fort Thompson
Red Beach One
San Carlos Sound
East Falkland
Sunday 30th May

Yer Fiddler,

As you can see by the address we are pleasantly ensconced here on the Beach-head. My Team have obtained a piece of real-estate and built their Fort and I have my 'house' inside. All are in good heart and bearing up in the conditions well.

My fiddle is the only instrument in the whole place and, on the way down, in demand at Church services and the like. Teapot is here and I have provided him with tobacco, rum and the bottle of chili sauce you asked me to get to him. Also bloater paste and anchovy paste to the Surgeons. He is now comfortable in a 'mick' which is a damn sight better than a concrete deck. We have had some music but have decided not to play the 'Downfall of Paris' until after dark as the last time we got air-raided and 4 dead. The building is made of cork which reduces rubble damage but is no great protection against stray rockets and cannon fire. My shelter station is the piss-house next to Fort Thompson's Triumphal Arch (sand-bags). Last night we got our first bit of snow and it seems that the weather is turning but apart from that and a couple of days of storm, we have had good weather. Everyone prays for low cloud as air attacks are less likely then. The two that got in the other day were from 15 that got zapped. From Argy prisoners we know that the San Carlos Water is known as Death Alley. However, the Army Rapiers are running out of petrol for their generators and are not always switched on. Thus some get through. But all in all it has been quite interesting. All are well and morale is high. Perhaps we shall move out soon but where and when I do not know. However it has been a superb reunion. People from all over.

See yez
Bernie

30th May, Sunday

Dear Ma,

This is a rather hurried note as we have just heard that there is a mail run going out in an hour and everyone is busy writing home. If you look at my last letter you will be able to work out where I am now, as I was right in my supposition of going further south for a salvage job. Obviously, being officially in the 'war zone', I can give no actual details but suffice to say that we have been working quite hard and are glad to be doing something at last. All the lads are in good heart and enjoying the Island despite the fierce wind and the cold. I hope to get the chance to do a bit of walking locally, not that there is much of an area to do so, and, in the brief time we have been here, have found it all quite interesting. You would never believe the sheer size of Elephant Seals. I think Bruno-dog would be quite terrified of them.

It looks like we will be stuck here for a bit but I'll make sure that the lads don't get bored by finding them interesting things to do. We do seem a bit cut off from everything, though. So I'll get this in the mail to you right away and write again when I can.

Bye for now,
  Love from
    Nigel.

31.5.82 Monday
Piggy and half team away in the Geminis to locate and buoy *Antelope* and blow the *Ambuscade* bomb. The lads were a bit slow and not away until gone 1300. The rest of the team spent the day clearing out a mess deck behind the Blast wall for our use, shifting gear and sorting out Fort Thompson. This took all day. Met Michael Nicholson and Brian Hanrahan ashore, filming the Argy prisoners coming ashore. A right sorry lot. Life here is getting very trench warfare-ish with black mud everywhere, but at least we are comfortable compared to the front line troops.

The prisoners were herded inside this eve as the temp out has been falling to minus 5°C and deaths were feared. Space was limited due to the bomb rooms being evacuated, so 400 of them were put in two small rooms 30' × 20', sat in rows, real tight together. They suffered from heat, as did we in the next door mess, and condensation, but all survived which they would not have done outside.

MUD

As curved as an eastern slipper
The black, glue-like San Carlos peat
Clings to the toe-cap of my boot
And overlays the camouflage
That renders me invisible.
Cracking like a blood-stiff bandage
Each puttee, steeped in quagmire ooze,
In loosing, shows the cloth beneath
As brightly clean and livid as
The pink of newly healing wounds.

This was a bad and uncomfortable night. It is amazing how much heat can be generated by a large number of closely packed bodies.

As it was very cold outside and there was no shelter for our Argy prisoners, it was decided to herd them inside for the night. Space was extremely limited and consequently a sort of 'Black Hole of San Carlos' situation developed. The Royal Marine special linguist prisoner-handlers led them in about 20 at a time. I have seen film of First World War gas victims in the trenches: long lines of sightless men, hand on the shoulder of the man in front, shuffling, convict-like, in a crocodile, led by the sighted. This was the same. Sad-faced, even terrified young men, heads bowed in the same hopeless attitude, shuffling with chain-gang dejection through the Stygian gloom of the old refrigeration plant, to be sat in row upon row, silent but at least warm.

More and more shrugged past and disappeared into the nether regions of the building. The heat increased through the night until sleep was impossible. The smell of those close-packed bodies was of a stomach-turning order and we were no roses ourselves, I should imagine. By two in the morning there arose the serious consideration of whether to knock a hole in the wall to let the heat out and the air in. Everything was running with condensation and breathing was a chore. After all, the building was steel frame filled with cork blocks skinned with cement; it should be easy to break through, a matter of a couple of minutes and then blissful fresh air. But no, we are trained not to do anything as radical, anything as sensible, without permission; and who is going to wake the Senior Officer to get that permission? Not I, sir!

Or perhaps sense prevailed. After all, better hot and clammy than cold, damp and hypothermic. We survived. It was not pleasant, but we survived.

The next night the prisoners were put in the evacuated spaces and were thus more comfortable. Well, after all, they were their bombs.

PRESERVATION

Sink slowly into green and windswept hills,
Whose purple rocks are buttresses of truth.
Defy the cunning, soul-ensnaring ills
And leave them chase their vigil after youth.
Let passions fly, nor yet your will enfold
But join the creatures of the moors and streams.
Think their thoughts, their freedom always hold;
Make this belief the lynchpin of your dreams.
Protect it in the mantle of your heart
And walk where only others' thoughts can be.
Allow your capture – so to 'come its part
And thus, in such communion, set you free.

1.6.82 Tuesday
Hot as hot on waking and everything damp. Argies moving out at 1000. No breakfast now but brunch instead.

Last night, as we were watching the Argy prisoners shuffling their endless way into the messdecks, Major Tony Nott (backed by the Colonel) told the lads something that we never realised. If *Lancelot* and *Galahad* had remained out of use or had blown up, the whole operation would have possibly failed. Certainly it was hanging on a knife edge at the time.

A bit worried about one of the team. He is terrified of bombs and therefore useless for shifting them. He actually shakes.

Today the lads got the plaque off the front of *Antelope* (sunk). Whiskey and John Boy recovered it under Piggy's supervision. Good effort. Tomorrow may-be the bell. I was aboard *Intrepid* for rocket-wrench instruction and *Fearless* for briefing. [A rocket wrench is used to remove a fuse from a bomb so fast that it has not time to realise that it is being interfered with and to react accordingly; by the time it has, it is out and away and impotent.] Team blew up a UXB on the fore-shore in a spectacular plume of water just on supper time. Argy prisoners looked like corn in a high wind as they threw themselves to the deck. They were herded inside again tonight but luckily managed to put half of them in the mess between bombs and blast wall.

One of the LCTs had found the last of the unaccounted bombs from the Great Raid by the effective method of all but sitting on it at low water. There it could be seen, just off the stern, lurking in the shallows.

When blowing such a beast to the nether world, it is wise to have some method of containing the blast and shrapnel. Sea water is an excellent medium for this and we worked out that, at the height of the tide, not only would we have enough water to do the job effectively but just the right depth to provide a spectacular column of spray going straight up into the air for a considerable distance. This would be well worth a photograph.

The charges were placed by a Diver using mask and snorkel, and all was ready for our exciting display. Everyone was gathered to watch it. Most people were down the way a bit, but some were up by the Argy compound, near the RAF bomb-team Land Rover. The signal was given, the charge initiated and up went the column of water, straight as a die, to disappear into the heavens. Several things happened at this point:

1. All the prisoners threw themselves flat to the deck, like a stack of dominoes being knocked over. It appears that they had either not received or not understood the message that there was going to be a 'bang' at that time.
2. The door of the normally-steamed-up and very stationary RAF Land Rover flew open and there appeared, ashen-faced, our overweight friend of the *Lancelot* recce, the one who elected to stay in the Gemini all night. It seems that his oppos had not told him about the 'bang' either.
3. A great round of applause from the assembled multitude greeted Numbers 1 and 2 and the 'bang' itself. Everyone was very taken with the event and returned to work happier and in high spirits.

PIPS

Officers' badges,
Frequently indistinct on
Camouflage parkas,
Become buried by action.
Rank holds no structure, except
To enhance the spur
Of natural leadership.

2.6.82 Wednesday
Not such a bad night due to more widely spaced prisoners. In fact really quite good.

After brunch, Piggy plus I plus Dave [our maintainer of engines and other gear] plus three lads went to *Fearless*. Gave the *Antelope* Plaque to the Captain, who received it with great reverence and locked it in his drawer. On meeting him, he said to us, 'I am very proud to meet you – very proud.'

What can you say to that? Managed to get six crates of beer for the lads and some softies. Back at Red Beach the Argies [prisoners] are on their way. RM Officers arrived from *Bedivere* (narrowly missed by 2 Exocets, apparently). Good to see them still alive.

The Team managed to sink the lifting bag on *Antelope*'s Oerlicon gun [20mm quick-firing cannon]. God knows how. Good meal at galley this eve. Party in the mess started slow but got going well in later stages.

Taff Hurley, who wanted to photo a dead body, was told of an Argy prisoner who had died and was in a body bag in one of the outbuildings. Shown by Phil Kearns where it was, he had second thoughts at the last minute about unzipping the bag for a photo, especially when Tommo leapt out of the bag at him! Great hilarity. TEAPOT INAUGURATED INTO THE LOG [the Grand Order of the Log: an informal Plymouth-based society devoted to good food, good ale, good music and good friends] BY 100% OF MEMBERS PRESENT (e.g. Grand Master). FULL CEREMONY TO BE CARRIED OUT ON RETURN TO GUZ.

So, much beer drunk, music, jokes, stories. Everyone to bed happy, including 4 × RM Seniors who are staying the night.

Taff Hurley, a keen and accomplished photographer, never went anywhere without his camera. He was determined to build up his own portfolio of his experiences and, when not engaged on other duties, sought out the best shots to take. The body bag incident indicates a certain unpredictability in the sense of humour of Divers and the rough and tumble with which they kid each other. Taff was serious enough about his photography to miss the signs and fall for a beautiful, instant spoof.

Later, on the return to the UK, everyone wanted to look at Taff's photos and get copies. Unfortunately it is sometimes difficult to keep track of who has borrowed what from whom and where it has been temporarily passed subsequently – and whose are those photographs anyway? This is particularly true if you are working in an on-call bomb team, and this is what happened to Taff's folio. He lent it out to people who, in the best of faith, lent it to others, and so on, until no one knew just who it belonged to. Some of his shots ended up in the national newspapers.

Somewhere out there is the recipient of the no doubt substantial remuneration for those pictures. He knows they are not his, and he was probably not even there. How about letting Taff have his folio back, eh? You'll find him c/o The Superintendent of Diving, HMS *Nelson*, Portsmouth.

3.6.82 Thursday
Piggy and I out as instructed for brief on board *Fearless* at 1000. Loch devoid of ships except for the *Canberra*, looking ghost-like in the dawning.

Before even dawn broke, Piggy and I were off in the Gemini to look for *Fearless*. Slowly the deeper shadows dissolved and one realised quite suddenly that light had returned to the scene. As yet there was no colour, only shades of grey, as we headed out into San Carlos Water in search of our quest.

The water was glass-smooth; not a ripple, not a feather of wind, but the mist hung in patches, wraith-like, all around. We left the engine locked to tend itself and both stood in tandem amidships. If we leant to the right, the boat would describe a gentle turn to starboard; if to the left, a similar turn to port. So we proceeded into that silent stillness, disappearing into the haze in great sweeping arcs. There was not a ship to be seen, no indication that we were anything other than the only ones alive in this corner of the world; just us, the boat, the engine and the mist.

Colour started to return and the toggle on Piggy's life-jacket became red, no longer grey. The shore line showed us browns and greens and . . . there . . . behind the edge of that mist curtain to port . . . was that the bow of a ship? A white ship ... *Canberra*. Seeming deserted in the still of the morning, she loomed above us, quite stationary, dirty-white and brown with rust streaks.

We hailed her. No reply. A complete circle of the hull and further calls still provoked no response. There was no other ship in sight, just the huge, ghostly bulk of *Canberra*, silent, aloof and alone.

We turned away and, still standing amidships, headed for home – for Red Beach. When we looked back, there was just the empty lough and its patches of mist. Nothing moved. Nothing showed. Neither of us spoke until we reached the shore and returned to the reality of tangible, speaking people, colour and bustle. But we HAD seen her. She HAD been there. Hadn't she?

No wind, glassy water. Back for breakfast before away to F at midday. Tasked to check Argy Ammo ship for 'Booby-traps' in Darwin. Looking forward to it.

Unfortunately the helo never turned up and the job is cancelled until tomorrow., Managed to get a bigger shoulder bag for survival kit and added to and repacked it. One 20mm gun recovered from *Antelope* and put on another of the 'A' boats [Type 21 frigates]. In the evening I was invited to bring my fiddle to the medical 'bar'. Played and did cabaret with Teapot. All the usual things. Good results too. Bloody hell, the whiskey flows like water round here!

4.6.82 Friday
Waited all day to go to Darwin which did not happen. The team got off the 2nd Oerlikon (snaffled by *Avenger* almost before clearing the water) and the *Antelope* deck plate. Not much else. 5 in No FCDT 1 arrived in broke Gemini in eve. I'm getting a cold.

Much of the Team's time was spent diving on the hull of HMS *Antelope* with the intention of recovering weapons, destroying such explosives as torpedoes and reducing the height of the wreck to allow safe passage of our ships. They were currently restricted in their movement by the huge area of water around the wreck which had been designated as a danger zone and was likely to remain so until FCDT 3 had completed their clearance of the hull.

The Oerlikon 20mm guns that were removed were eagerly grabbed by any ship in the know and mounted as extra anti-aircraft defence, much needed at that time. One was snaffled by *Avenger*, almost before the thing had cleared the water, mounted swiftly upon their superstructure and named 'Antelope's Avenger'.

As a bonus, if you like, between such tasks, the Divers also removed both ceremonial deck plates from the gangways and the ship's crest from the front of the bridge. These were given to the COs of *Fearless* and *Intrepid* for safe keeping.

One of *Antelope*'s deck plates was presented later to her affiliated Sea Cadet unit, TS VAGA in Hereford, where I had been an instructor years before. It was unfortunate that none of FCDT 3 were informed of this presentation. On finding out about the occasion unofficially, the Divers who actually recovered the 'trophy' were specifically told that they would not be welcome at the ceremony but could attend in the crowd at their own expense. That hit the boys hard and saddened them considerably, particularly considering the risk they underwent at the time.

5.6.82 Saturday
Turned in all day with flu. In a bad way. Made it to breakfast, but only just.

Since the destruction of the Corporal Chef's galley in the bombing raid, he had moved it across to the other side of the valley where there was a hardstanding and some low breeze-block walling. Here he pitched his tents, set up his equipment and dispensed victuals.

Getting to Lenny's Cafe was a serious evolution. The first

obstacle was a stone-field that had to be crossed in the dark since, aware of the danger to large groups gathering in daylight, Len had decided that he would only feed people at dawn and dusk. As one stumbled across this tortuous labyrinth there was an overwhelming temptation to use a heavily shaded torch in order to avoid the worst pitfalls.

'Put that light out!' came the oft-repeated cry, and on one went, sightless and sore. All of a sudden the stone-field ended and walking was easier – until one fell into the bog. The progress of many boots had turned what had been a pretty, green, if treacherous, sward into a black, peaty quagmire that grew and grew with the passing of time and more boots.

However, having successfully negotiated these two hazards, one found oneself in close proximity to Len's Cafe and hot food. A quick scramble up on to the hard standing and there was the tent and a queue of hungry men.

Written in chalk on the canvas sides was the menu: Chicken Supreme/Surprise/Casserole or Stew/Hot Pot/Casserole (depending on the day), and Mashed Potato/Pomme de Terre Frappé/Duchess Potatoes/Spud Lyonnaise (depending on Lenny's mood).

For quite some time the menu remained the same: a spoonful of chicken supreme and one of 'pom'. Rations were short and variety difficult to arrange, though Len did wonders with what he had.

Then, having got one's scran, it was, 'B***** off you lot – I don't want to become a target!' and off we all b*****ed and sat around the tent in a great circle – but a good twenty feet clear. A couple of minutes later, it was back to the tent to dhobi one's dixie, and then the ankle-wrenching, wet, muddy stumble back to Fort Thompson, maybe sucking a sweet that Len had given out or perhaps crunching on a biscuit [A/B]. Joy indeed.

Gyro toppled [ill] and aching all over. Lads had bath and dhobi day.

6.6.82 Sunday
Much better this morning. Played (not very well) at church service. Urgent message, 'Get to *Fearless*!' V. bumpy ride in 'rigid raider' in bad weather [fast raiding boat used by the Royal Marines, rather like a modern dory; you will probably see a picture of one in the window of your RN recruiting office when you or your children go to sign-on]. Turned out to be no panic. Had lunch and bath aboard. Really was a day of rest apart from securing the boats. [Boats are normally hoisted in bad weather, but not in this time of hostilities; they consequently need tending and constant attention.] Still no advance on Stanley. 42 ['Four Two' Commando Royal Marines] and 2 Para dug in on a couple of hills in direct contact with the weather. Some lads had feet blown off by mines. John Boy discovered that he had worms late this eve. [He had been diving off an area of shore line where the Argy prisoners' effluent ran out.] Took him to the Docs to be purged. And it certainly purged him!

7.6.82 Monday
Breakfast cabaret this afternoon [we were still on UK time] was *Exeter* firing 2 × Sea Wolf [long range anti-aircraft missiles] from her anchorage. Got one aircraft, the other ran. Message from *Fearless* not to do the *Antelope* 'blatting' of the torpedos due to inclement weather. No news of tomorrow's trip to Darwin as yet. Apparently the pilot hit this morning was on our R/T net. They heard yattering, screaming and then silence. John Boy not well. Lads watching medical operations this afternoon. Team 'blatted' unidentified 'bit' from rocket on beach.

This evening at 1920 we buried four Army Air Corps men who were shot down yesterday (possibly by one of our ships) while setting up an OP at 0430 (or perhaps it was the day before). The service was carried out despite and during an 'air raid red' and with helos plying around the area. As the Padre said afterwards, 'At least we did it with dignity.' We were gathered atop the hill, surrounded by sangars, as the dusk settled and the distant mountains were shrouded in mist. Maybe a hundred were gathered in the rising wind. The service was simple and effective. Each one was laid to rest by 6 pall-bearers who saluted before turning away. No shots were fired. Then a Piper played 'Flowers of the Valley' ['Flowers of the Forest'] as most turned and left. Only the RN contingent were left when the fiddle started on 'The Dark Isle' as their own tribute [a lament of great sadness; the lads formed a human wall to windward of the fiddle to stop the bow being blown off the strings in the rising gale]. It was nice to see Michael Nicholson again, representing the Media at the Service.

Later in the evening, a switch-off tune at the mess tent for those collecting scran for the evening meal.

AT AJAX BAY

Legs lie crooked, but a fag don't help;
Bodies, shrouded with canvas tenting,
Hastily concealed, yet undisguised,
Struggle in vain for my attention.

Heavily pregnant with wounded men,
Camouflaged helos pass overhead,
Darting like birds of prey for the pad
And the medics of the life machine.

The down-draught tears the air to pieces.
Silent with the casualties' torment
Yet stunned by the engines' agonies,
It sets the ripped tarpaulin flapping.

The silver bodybags start shaking
As if their occupants, awakened
From a horrifying nightmare, were
In dread panic, thrashing to escape.

Later we shall bury them at dusk
And on the hill, a piper playing
'The Flowers of the Forest', gravely
And with the comradeship bid them farewell.

By now people had started to get a little bored with the daily diet of chicken supreme and 'pom', but that was all there was. Even 'nutty' (chocolate) was in short supply, having somehow mysteriously vanished from the ration packs between leaving UK and arriving at the BMA (Red Beach).

Lenny the chef decided that it was about time to liven up the dinner queue, and set about decorating the breeze-block walls round the galley tent with fronds of bracken. That evening, in the gloom of dusk, his customers were serenaded by the nearest he could get to a string quartet, that is BB and his fiddle, in the plush surroundings of the 'San Carlos Palm Court Hotel' (chalked on the side of the tent). As the dinner queue wound its way past the 'orchestra', from the inside of the entrance curtain could be heard the irregular 'clatter-clatter, chink-chink, rattle-rattle' of money falling on to a tin plate. On closer inspection there could be seen a legend chalked round the edge: 'Support the RNLI. You never know when you'll need one.' As the men went past, those with money threw it in and those without applauded enthusiastically.

On leaving the tent there could be seen, nestling among the bracken fronds protruding from the wall top, a small white object, pencilled upon which was: 'Yes, this IS an egg.'

Two days later eggs were on the menu. There is nothing quite so delicious as a fried egg after a diet of 'compo'; and one thing was certain, namely the answer to the question, 'Which came first, the chicken supreme or the egg?' (a local saying at the time).

CHICKEN SUPREME

By crossing the stone-field into the bog,
And heading en masse for Len's Cafe,
At dawn or at dusk, in drizzle or fog,
From vehicles, shelters, secure or unsafe,
Or the shingle-bag sangar we all improvise,
The Royals, the matelots ask with aplomb,
'So, what have you got for us?' – Lenny replies,
'Chicken Supreme and Pom!'

Although it comes natural, after a while,
To crave something different . . . . one learns;
From fiddle-tuned dinner queue, Lenny's broad smile
And passing the 'oeuf à la coque' in the ferns;
For the Lifeboat will prosper, and no cause to beg,
With money they threw in the plate for that prom -
But what was it followed the sight of the egg?
Chicken Supreme and Pom.

A Tank Landing Craft can be fetid and cold,
Abandoned without any power;
While UXBs, shifted by chain hoist, I'm told,
Can hold one's attention for hour after hour
But the candle-lit quiz, when invited to dine,
Since lifting and shifting the thousand-pound bomb,
'What feast can we have with that bottle of wine?'
'Chicken Supreme and Pom.'

'Chicken Supreme and Pom', says he,
'A spoonful of each – that's your lot.
There ain't nothing else, apart from the tea,
But it's tasty, nutritious and hot!'

Teapot came to the mess for the end of the day. John Boy still bad and moved at midnight to the hospital ward.

John Boy, who only ever wore training shoes on his feet, was struck down at about the same time that Joe Gofton, the youngest-looking of our Divers, was arrested under suspicion of being an escaped Argy prisoner.

John Boy had been diving close to the shore in an area contaminated by prisoner effluent, and a day or two later discovered that he had picked up 'worms'.

At the sick bay he was given a worm powder to get rid of the little blighters, and it damn near killed him. Whether it was an allergic reaction or what, we never knew, but on the night of the 7th he was moved into the hospital for close observation and careful nursing.

He recovered a few days later, and never once during his illness, nor indeed during the whole campaign, was he seen to be down or morose. Always one could rely on a smile from John Boy, and he became our mascot.

JOHN BOY

They say young John Boy's
On the danger list;
He'll be lucky to survive.
How bloody stupid,
All the risks he's run,
To be killed by a microbe.
He caught it diving
On a UXB
Next to the sewer.

They say young John Boy's
In the danger ward
And he's fighting for his life;
Yet, always smiling,
He hugs his trainers
To him, like a talisman.
Come on, John Boy!
You're our lucky mascot
You've got to pull through.

Monday 7th June
Red Beach One

Yer Fiddler!

At breakfast this morning we had a nice little cabaret when, with a couple of wooshes, the *Exeter* fired off two Sea Wolf missiles. It was only when the first one exploded, against what later was confirmed to be an Argy aircraft, and the second was aborted, that we got the air raid warning RED. However it was a good diversion from the first of the two compo meals of the day.

The Team has been diving on the burned-out wreck of the *Antelope* and managed to retrieve the crest off the bridge and the starboard deck plate for onward transmission to the Imperial War Museum and Naval Church. We have in fact been quite busy. At present we are living between 2 × 500lb UXBs and the Hospital, behind a blast wall of sandbags that we spent all night building. Not only do we reckon that this is the safest place, but it gives the medics confidence. Also, the Argy prisoners have only one dry place to be right under the two bombs; that is behind us. Don't they ever stink. Their Officers are right arrogant bastards too – or were. However a couple of things have brought them down a peg. One – the heads are in front of the troops, in plain view, and it does not matter how much you think of yourself, you all shit the same. Two – some prisoners arrived from Goose Green all shot up. They had been shifting ammo in a captured dump. They did not know that their Colonel had ordered it booby-trapped. So the Medics were patching them up but needed blood urgently. The Argies wanted to give it but their Colonel said, 'No.' So Surgeon Commander Jolly had him wheeled in to where they were operating on one of his men with both legs blown off. 'Tell him,' he said to the interpreter, 'that some bastard ordered the ammunition he was shifting to be booby-trapped and never told anyone. I've got fifteen more of these waiting for operations.'

Apparently the Colonel went white, and not only did they get 60 units of blood instant, but he also mapped out the bomb and mine sites for the RAF EOD Team to deal with. They're away doing that now.

The other evening, just at the right time as it turned out, the Medics invited me to play fiddle for them in their operating-theatre Bar. Teapot and I made it a sort of Cabaret evening and did a few of the old favourites. This eve, however, we are having a get-together to work out a few more. I was told later that it was just the boost they needed after some particularly heavy days. Fiddle also in demand for Services (various) [funerals]; some occur at odd hours and in desolate places.

I was 'down' with a 36-hr flu yesterday and the day before. A real hard hitter but am OK now. Otherwise so far we have been remarkably healthy. I have one of the lads down with the nasty after-effect of having been 'wormed'. He must have picked them up diving off the beach near the sewage outlet. Will have to watch that in future.

The air raids remain fairly constant above us and the weather is fluctuating from calm to force 8s and 9s.

Stanley is surrounded but the big push is yet to happen. The weather is not helping those in forward positions. However, I cannot say much about that here.

Could you please give Dickie Barr a ring and sitrep for me as there are not many of these letter forms around and we are rationed. I am writing only to you and Ma so hope you will keep all informed of the situation. Teapot and I thought of you yesterday afternoon and evening and both reckon that we are by proxy 'Jennings at War'. So you keep it going at home, Dad, and we'll sort it out, out here. Anyway, latest buzz is: 'Saturday night in the pub in Stanley and I'm playing fiddle, Boys!'

Bernie

Monday, June 7th

Dear Ma,

Another chance of a mail drop (they do come at infrequently odd times) and a chance to let you know how we are getting on.

This job we are on has turned out to be much more complicated than we at first thought and we are actually working quite hard. What hasn't helped is that I went down with flu a few days ago but am OK now. One of the lads, John Boy, has gone down with a nasty viral infection but seems to be fighting it off – fingers crossed.

The Team is quite superb. I mean, here we are, miles from anywhere, with all this stuff to do and only the briefest contact with the outside world, yet their morale is as high as that and we all get on very well. They really are a great bunch. I feel honoured to be their Boss. It is at times like this that one realises just how good they are.

I see that things in the Falklands are progressing well, though they have had their set-backs; but you will no doubt know all about that through the news bulletins. I should think that we shall not be here too much longer.

I hope that all is well with you and that Bruno-dog is well settled in by now.

Best love,
Nigel

AT THE RED AND GREEN LIFE MACHINE
(unfinished)

He was bathing in a pint of tepid water
And shaving in the remnants of his tea.
Coldly standing in a bucket in the passage
Was the Triage Dental Surgeon's nudity.

Sleeping soldiers packed the corridors and crossings,
While Divers dumped the sandbags by the wall
Where an unexploded bomb lodged in the ceiling
And another in the 'frigeration stall'.

For a hammock slung between the meathook girders
Can host a brief, impromptu cabaret,
But it is not easy writing home a 'bluey'
When the nearest light is twenty feet away.

With a pocket full of rum and one of whisky,
In a cammy-jacket's mottled brown and green,
Comes the bear-like three-ring-Surgeon titleholder
Of Rick Jolly's multicoloured Life Machine.

Keep your head down, mate!
Until this raid is over;
I would not have your job -
Not if you paid.

Keep your head down, mate!
Until the night conceals us
Or 'Warning Red' plays
'Yellow's' serenade.

8.6.82 Tuesday
Writing this outside CP Bunker during Red Alert at 1920. Many choppers bringing in wounded from *Galahad* and *Plymouth*. Tommo plus team out on *Antelope* still but late blowing the Torpedos. Piggy and I, having been

briefed in *Fearless* for future jobs plus Team's next move. Dory engine only going astern on way back. Taff, driving, got very wet. Red alert then too. O/A [on arrival] Red Beach called to blow rocket on North Ridge.

2 × blow on job, no high order. Now waiting for the *Antelope* blow and forecast air attack from West Falkland.

The rocket that we had to blow on North Ridge had landed close to a couple of Royal Marine trenches. Within the nearest were Rick Willers and his oppo, busily frying potatoes on a camp stove. Where he got them from is a mystery, for he still will not tell me to this day. Well, he had to move. That trench was definitely too close to the impending explosion.

'No, you carry on,' declared the occupants, 'we'll just keep our heads down.' And they continued to concentrate on the, by now tantalisingly, aromatic spuds.

Having been enlightened that we wanted to use their trench as bunker for the 'blow' and that there was not room enough for us all, they departed for the other sangar, carrying their stove with the potatoes still cooking upon it.

Clearance Divers know Royal Marines and Royal Marines know Clearance Divers, and no one was going to leave anything lying around. After all, the potatoes might have been knocked over and buried by a falling clod of earth, had they been left in situ. That would have been tragic.

In the previous few days we had been visited at Red Beach by 16 Field Ambulance, an Army medical unit, who had arrived girt about in immaculate webbing gear, tin-hatted and shiny-booted, from an LCU.

Marching in ranks, stern faced and in perfect formation, they were led by an officer with a leonine head of grey hair and more pouches and packs than one had the right to imagine. Whilst his men waited in ranks outside, this officer, much encumbered by his over-large girth of equipment, was shown the hospital facility and operating theatre, much to the delight and amusement of anyone lucky enough to witness the scene.

Then, presumably told that they were not required in that particular location, the whole lot of them turned and marched back down to the beach, still in ranks, only this time they were smiling.

2330
The operating theatres have been going full blast. Carnage – apparently. The Lads have been magnificent; carrying stretchers, dressing burns and generally nursing. We all did our bit. *Galahad* is gone. *Plymouth* we think is OK (fires out but 2 × UXBs on board). *Sir Tristram* hit. 2 companies of Welsh Guards were lost/or believed lost in *Sir G*. She was unloading at the time, her bow door open but blocked by a broken LSU which also went. [This later turned out to be spurious information and untrue.] The soldiers were unloading phosphorous grenades and front line ammunition. I think the heaviest losses yet. Also all of 16 Ambulance's kit went down.

Our boys helping generally in the ward, also with operations (holding open wounds to be stitched). Finished eventually around 0200. Comment from Colonel, 'They are the scruffiest sailors I've ever seen, but they make wonderful nurses and thank God they're here.'

That's the front line hospital gone. This will have a profound effect on the attack. The Argies have played the classic lulling game with enough feints to keep things ticking before a big hit. We are more vulnerable now as half the Rapier emplacements have gone to the front line.

Most of the casualties were burn cases though a significant number were mangled. Our mess now half filled with Chogie survivors [Chinese crew from the LSLs].

The *Antelope* blow got as far as severing the whip aerial before becoming a miss-fire. Piggy to finish tomorrow. Maybe we will move to *Lancelot* then or perhaps it will all change. We shall see. *Inshallah* [Arabic; 'May it be the will of Allah'] not another night/day like this.

With Bluff Cove came the justification of the Team's forethought in attending medical lectures and operations over the past weeks. Straight away they were able to relieve the medics of much of the lesser work, thus releasing them to more important jobs. Some helped out in the theatre but most took charge of the burn victims and with infinite gentleness dressed their ghastly wounds and eased their pain. What finer accolade could they have than for Colonel Ivor Helberg to have made that wonderful statement that ended, 'And thank God they're here.'

Others of the Team ministered to the many survivors coming in and FCDT 3's remaining stocks of clothing were distributed amongst the ill-dressed ships' companies of the two LSLs. Most of these were Chinese from Hong Kong, the traditional crews of these ships, but one young Brit stood out a mile. His hair, which had been thick, had fused like a helmet round his head and he was blackened about the face and hands.

Those who have seen on television the film of the men coming ashore at Bluff Cove will have noticed this young man in the background. In the film he is wearing a pair of blue overalls, such as Stokers have. When he arrived with us, all he wore were boots and a pair of underpants. He had given his overalls away to a less fortunate comrade between leaving Bluff Cove and reaching San Carlos.

A sailor from *Plymouth* also grabbed the attention and admiration of the team: although badly wounded himself, he was greatly concerned for his oppo, wounded in the head, next to him.

CASUALTIES

> The stretchered sailor, by his friend
> Whose hand he clasped and willed his pain to mend,
> In whispers to a medic, raised
> Imploring eyes, whose sparkle morphine glazed,
> Said, 'Help my oppo, please, not me.
> He's hurting bad, and worse – he cannot see.'

9.6.82 Wednesday
Up at 0900. Sent message to *Fearless* that Team for Fitzroy Bridge and volunteers for EOD on *Sir T* (2 × UXB) ready at first light. (Tommo, Jock Rebecca, Whiskey)

Just how does one pick men to do a dangerous job? In the MCD Branch, the boss is always the first man in when tackling an 'explosive' situation; as facts become clearer and the dangers are known, so more people are involved. In diving it works the other way. The Diver does the recce and as the situation becomes more complicated, so the more expert rate or rank is called for.

Galahad was easy; the boss would do the job and with him men he chose, preferably not married and without ties. Then came *Lancelot*. Here the CPO took over with his hand-picked team, but not those who had already 'had a go'. Now the Fitzroy Bridge job tied up the remainder, and they were on stand-by to move.

The Bluff Cove ships needed looking at. Volunteers from the first two teams were called for and it was the boss's turn to lead them on. No one can put down hard and fast rules about who should be picked in these situations. People step forward. They are all first-class men. It is enough.

On to *Fearless* at first light. *Sir Tristram* and *Sir Galahad* too far gone for immediate EOD. Perhaps later. Immediate task is *Antelope*'s Torps. Chief doing that (Piggy Trotter].

Chris Meatyard and I went off to *Cordella* (trawler) to meet with Martin Holloway plus two skippers (*Pict* and *Funnella* (?)). Red alert ended that meeting. Returned via Piggy who's having trouble finding 'A' [*Antelope*]. Sent Phil and Wheels to help. Trawler COs on board F for a brief. Met Mike and Brian TV in W/R. Mike asked me to name the tune I played at the funeral t'other night. Told him it was 'The Dark Isle' and we caught up on news.

The blow on A cancelled again! due to *Fearless* not being able to move during an air raid as she had to cover Red Beach. [Since the bombing, there was always a ship just off shore to protect the hospital.] The MCM conference was more MCM than D [Mine Counter Measures and Diving] and out of my scope. Anyway I was called away to tell F to move as she was too close to the blast. Piggy has wired up 6 × torpedo and 4 × Sea Cat.

Should be good when it eventually goes. In the eve I played fiddle in the mess. Teapot came plus Steve and bottle of rum. Steve is pre-Big Eric medic on Diego [Diego Garcia, a tiny island in the Indian Ocean with a small RN party and many Americans on it]. Knows Fids. Saw off the bottle between us and ditted [spun yarns to each other; from 'ditty']. Crashed out around 0100.

'See you around. Keep your head down.' This is fast becoming the Falklands Farewell.

10.6.82 Thursday

1325. On the helo-run close to the ground over the barren, rolling, boggy Falkland hills. A stream of helos to our left coming back from the SE, us part of a stream heading there. The Blow yet again cancelled. Team moving to *Sir Lancelot*. Tommo, Whiskey, Jock plus I aloft in a Sea King [Sea King helicopter] on our way to *Sir Tristram*.

The two LSLs *Tristram* and *Galahad* are anchored in a pleasant, low lying inlet both with superstructures burned out and G still burning from the tank deck. A sad, sad sight. We were winched onto *Sir T* [also burning aft] and started the search. One 500lb bomb had passed through from stbd quarter to port quarter, another had entered forward of that and exploded in the tiller flat, bowing the deck and venting upward through a space to starboard and out through the 1st bomb exit hole. The superstructure, largely alloy, had burned and melted away but the rest of the ship was perfect. [The molten metal had run under the fire doors and had set in a petrified waterfall down the ladders to the midship accommodation.] After some discussion with 2 officers from *Sir Lancelot*, we attempted to get stern doors then bow doors open. No go, so blew the stern chains and she fell open in the water. Meanwhile someone had rifled through my kit and nicked my hip flask full of rum. Bastards! Percy Pongo, I suspect, for they were on board rabbiting. We had quiet evening in one of the mess decks though it was cold.

THE DERELICT

She lies as lies the rabbit or the doe,
With broken back and rapid shallow breath,
Who rises even yet before its foe
And shouts defiance, shouts it unto death.

She lies and cries from pity and from shame,
Looks up to give a blind and helpless call
Whose answer echoes, calling out her name,
'No one will come, no help will come at all.'

She lies and sighs so lonely in the dawn,
Her bulkheads at the mercy of the tide,
Her lifeboats gone, their ladders left forlorn
Which slowly swing and scratch and scratch her side.

> She lies and dies, she sees the waves advance
> And waits to feel them wash her life away;
> Until the long grey ships her pleas entrance
> And softly come to help her on her way.

The feeling of jumping on to a deserted, burning ship, in which it is believed there lurk unexploded bombs, is a weird one. Not for nothing did the Sea King pilot balk at touching down. Descending from the door of the helo on to the deck seemed like passing from one world to another. Up there we were looked after, we could go away. Once on the deck we were committed. They winched us down, and we were on our own.

Whiskey, who had been part of the Big Bad Bomb removal team, took Jock 2 and went away to search the forward two-thirds of the ship. There, in the mess-decks and cabins, they found a 'Marie Celeste' situation that indicated instant flight. Personal kit was left where it lay: passports, wallets, tape recorders, books, writing gear and the like. There was no damage, just absolute stillness.

Where Tommo and I went it was different. The stern superstructure had been burned to a shell and was indeed still burning. Most of the screens and bulkheads had been melted away and just the framework and some plate remained. No way to get down there. We would have to approach from within, from the forward compartments.

Reaching the big fire-doors that separated the after section from the embarked accommodation, we found the way impassable yet again. The doors, which were designed to close automatically in the event of fire, had done just that, and had saved the fore part of the ship from any kind of damage; but there was something else.

Great petrified waterfalls of molten alloy, the last vestige of the missing superstructure decks, and mute witness to the enormous heat that had destroyed them, lay hanging off the steps to those doors, under which the metal had flowed like a river.

We went deeper and eventually penetrated into the

machinery complex. Dark it was and cold: quite silent and with that peculiar smell so redolent of a dead ship. Splitting the spaces between us for a more effective search, we parted on our separate ways, and yet I always knew where Tommo was and he always knew my position. We could not see each other as we penetrated the many different compartments, neither could we hear anything; for we were being quite silent, listening and looking. But we knew. Surrounded in the darkness by great engines and machines, pipes, ladders, walkways and tanks, we searched by torchlight: quite alone, subdued by the silence of sleeping monsters, deep in the bowels of the ship, knowing that the deeper we went the more impossible would be escape in an emergency; listening, listening. We peered everywhere for anything that would indicate the presence of a lurking one-thousand-pounder, and waited for the explosion we were expecting. That was loneliness indeed.

But what was the light ahead? It was Tommo, who had finished his half as I completed mine. All clear.

Back on deck there were now several folk around and waiting to go below. Their officer pointed out that gear must be collected and the personal kit of those who had been on board must be returned to them. As there were no UXBs to be found on board, this permission was given and we turned to the next task.

Captain Roy Southworth RAOC, whose area we were in, was desperate to get at the ammunition carried in the hold. As he pointed out, the bombardment of the Stanley defences was on and the guns were hungry. With the help and advice of two RFA officers, Tommo and I had a look at the stern ramp-door but found it jammed fast in the closed position. The bow doors and ramp were designed to open by gravity but refused. Everything astern was burned or still burning, but I divined that we could perhaps open the drawbridge-like back door by severing the chains that raised it and now held it fast. Thus it would be allowed to fall flat to the water. A friendly Royal Engineers Para appeared at this time with a bag full of plastic explosive, and once again we undertook the perilous journey along the starboard side of the burned out shell. When one is faced with such a traverse, a life spent mountaineering certainly helps, and rock climbing expertise comes into its own.

Treading warily on rotten, burned out struts and plating, moving up, down or along, wherever there was a way, sometimes hanging over the side or above some smoking black hole by arms alone, we moved slowly aft, carrying the explosives on our backs. Through the stench of still-burning fires we raised clouds of ash in the motionless air. Everywhere there was ash, black, white and grey, coating every surface and turning us into chimney-sweeps.

Reaching the after chain-deck, we soon had the cutting charges ready, although the soot and ash and our limited equipment did not make it that easy to keep them in place. But it was done. Now the traverse back, only this time reeling out the 'electric string' behind us so that we could detonate from a safe distance. Who could tell how that vitrified superstructure would react to another explosion?

Karrumpettah! Sperlash! Perfect. The chains parted cleanly. The door hinged down to splash flat on the water, then slowly sank until it was hanging vertically below the stern. The way was open and the last stock of ammunition was available for collection. Or was it? There was still a fire burning to port and the ammo would have to be carried past it. Straight away the four of us set about fighting the fire and soon had the flames out. The burning compartment turned out to be the wardroom wine store, and we were able to move much of the stock to a lock-up formed by a stairwell with a fire-buckled door at the top and a well hammered clip-set [door] at the bottom. There it remained safe until handed over to an RFA Officer the next day. He was very decent about it and offered us our pick, so we took some 'prezzies' back for the lads.

Back on the deck, dusk was settling in the stillness of the evening as we retrieved our personal gear from the starboard Bofors magazine, where we had left it neatly stowed at the start of the day. Now no longer neat, and no longer stowed, it was strewn around the compartment having been well rifled and all good things removed, including my hip-flask of rum. I wonder what sort of person steals his fellow's personal possessions while he is away doing highly dodgy things, particularly in such a harsh environment. There certainly are some weird people about.

Night came and we retired to a mess-deck for shelter. I never realised just how cold a dead ship could be until that night. We found some extra bedding in a store close by, but even so that was a desolate place to stay. Ships are always full of noise and vibration. This one was silent as the grave and just as chilly. We passed an uneasy night.

TRISTRAM AT THE COVE

It was all too easily definite.
All it required was to take our kit
Into a twisted ship and climb
Ladders and walkways, a step at a time,
Down and through her cavernous bowels,
Ignoring the damage's groans and growls,
Past the engines, looming and damp,
With only the warmth of a battery lamp,
Hanging from girders blackened with soot,
Gauging the strength of the plates underfoot,
Thoroughly, doggedly, further apart,
When all you can hear is the beat of your heart,
Finding the source of the havoc to know
That nothing else lurked and was waiting to blow,
Cautiously peering in corners to see,
Silently searching – Tommo and me.

11.6.82 Friday
Having been promised a helo at 1300, of course it never turned up. We have mustered a palatte load of gear, by arrangement with *Sir T* Officer, inc a 35hp outboard

engine, to go back and no way will we be separated from it. So we guard our kit. Even so our bedding and rations had disappeared by the evening from the mess! Percy Pongo again. An LCU [Unspecified Landing Craft] from *Intrepid* arrived with rum and breakfast. Very welcome. [We had been standing in the back door-opening feeling cold and hungry, when he came at us waving a bottle and indicating food: what a thoughtful fellow.] Later the Commander E from *Fearless* arrived with a team. Sorted him out OK.

Tommo and I went across to *Sir Galahad*. All burned out and still burning. Managed to recover 12 boxes of phosphorus grenades and some small arms. Found a young soldier dead on the upper deck. He had been in the prone position when killed and the heat of the fire had arched his shoulders and head off the deck. Boots and overboots still intact and some clothing on arms and right shoulder. Bottom of flesh burned away and stuck to deck. Back of legs, buttocks and back still in very good condition and skin undamaged and firm. Not falling to bits yet though would rip apart if a lift attempted. Needs shovelling off deck. Head burned, face gone, jaw bone open on right side. Hair still intact though somewhat frizzed on stbd side. No recognisable features. No dog tags visible. Hands roasted and ruddy. Top two joints of digits burnt away. We covered him with a blanket to keep the chill off, weighted it down and left him with his ship. He was only a young lad. About Joe Gofton's height (small) and now he's dead. Poor lad. [A detailed report was forwarded to the proper people.]

81 Ordnance Company have been doing all the rabbiting. Cameras have disappeared, cabins broken open and drawers. Yesterday there was money loafing everywhere. Today – nothing. RX gear [receiving gear, e.g. radios, tape recorders] that runs by battery has gone too. Everyone's personal gear has been turned over. Bad that!

Eventually managed to get a chopper out and it returned to get our gear afterwards. Piggy and team out doing a job on *Engadine*'s screw after blowing the A [*Antelope*'s torpedoes]. Rest of team still at Red Beach. Bar open. Padre visited. Teapot visited. All asleep by 0100.

What a welcome sight it was to see the 'big fella' in his LCU waving a bottle of rum. While we were inspecting the inside of it, breakfast was prepared for us and we soon hoovered that back.

Just astern lay *Galahad*. Smoke still rose from her main hatch and muffled explosions could be heard from time to time within her hull. Lifeboat falls hung dejected down her sides.

Whiskey and Jock set to work collecting the gear we needed to keep the Team operational. The RFA officers of the day before had been most helpful in this respect. Tommo and I set off to see what we could do for *Galahad*.

On board all was left in confusion. Fire had swept most of her and half-burned equipment lay strewn around the decks. The main hatch was open but nothing could be seen within owing to the smoke. There was nowhere we could go but the tank- and shade-decks, and little that we could salvage except a rigid raider-dory, an outboard motor, some grenades and some small arms. The doors of some compartments were blistered and smoking as fires still lurked inside.

The finding of the young lad touched us both deeply, and, having noted the facts of his situation, we gently covered him over and left him with his mates.

We were taken off by one of the lifeboats that had come off shore to do just that. This was achieved by our shinning down the boat's falls. Back on board *Sir Tristram*, Whiskey had disturbing news. Those who had come on board to 'collect people's personal papers, etc.' seemed to have gone about it in a peculiar way, for only the money and portable valuables had been removed. ID cards, passports, wallets and anything run by mains electricity had been left behind. All locked doors had been forced, and in the ship's RSM's cabin every drawer and locker had been broken into. No longer a 'Marie Celeste', the place had been ransacked, burgled and vandalised. We checked our kit and found that all our bedding and rations had disappeared. We had been done over twice in two days, and not by the enemy.

We mustered all our remaining gear and the stuff we had been allowed to collect, and netted it on to a pallet in the middle of the deck. From now on we always had a sentry on watch there. Finally, we removed the ship's crest from the front of the sagging bridge, a fair feat of mountaineering in itself. Later we got it to the Captain, who at that time possessed nothing but the contents of a survivor's emergency kit.

Eventually a helo arrived to take us back, and returned for the gear and sentry. We had learned a lot in those two days and sad was our meeting with our old friend *Galahad*. It was sadder still that we could do little to aid her; but she was a tough old bird and still rode high in the water. Her looks may have gone but her spirit was as defiant as ever.

TO A YOUNG GALAHAD

Naked is no way to die, nor yet to lie
Frozen in the act of living;
At first I thought you caught in spasm,
Locked into a callisthenic dorsal arch,
Muscles – shoulder, thigh and arm -
Straining with the effort.
Then I saw your face half burned away to show
The grin of teeth that lies beneath the skin,
Your fingers burned to stubby stumps
And dog-tags gone;
Only your boots and one arm thrust
Into a shirt marked your haste to leave.

(Did you once sun yourself, running your hand
Lazily over some girl-friend's thigh
As she in turn smoothed oil upon your back?)
Somehow you died whole, unbroken
Until you tumbled to that griddle deck
That burned and scorched and seared,
Welding you to it.
Who was the man that caused your death?
Was he like those who yesterday
Pilfered all our kit, while we
Hunted bombs and rockets
Deep in a dying ship?
Your ship is dying too, burning,
Rumbling to the explosions that
Rock the pall of blackened flames.
I cannot help her.
Excuse me if I leave you now
But there are jobs to do and fires to fight.
Snow is in the air and bleakness coming
With the winter wind.
Although you can feel nothing, yet
This trap will keep away the chill
And clothe you for a while from prying
Vulture eyes.
I leave you with your ship
To guard as you have done in lonely vigil;
But I will tell them where you lie
And, if tardily, someone will come
To tend you.

Arriving back at Red Beach after dark and reunited with our hard won gear, we received a meesage:

'Lenny wants ter see yer!'

Well, when summoned to Len's Cafe, one did not hesitate. There could be an extra spoonful of 'pom' in it or maybe even a 'baby's head' (tinned steak and kidney pudding, circa 1942). What a treat that would be.

Once past the stone-field and through the bog, we

squelched our way to the galley tent and called out our approach. Sweeping aside the tent flap, Lenny revealed to our gaze a full dinner for four, complete with wine and candles.

'Lenny, you're a bloody marvel!' we said – and say so still.

12.6.82 Saturday
JACK WOZ HERE '82
ROYAL NAVY
(Message left on the wall after Fort Thompson was dismantled and moved to *Lancelot*.) Played fiddle during loading. Really with it and played well. On moving off the Cox'n hoisted the Jolly Roger and I went onto the roof to play. We went round *Fearless* who clapped and cheered and took photos (including the Captain) so it was a <u>GOOD THING</u> TO HAVE DONE.

Colin Garwood says it was my idea but I seem to remember that he suggested it. He had brought his LCU in to move FCDT 3 and Fort Thompson to *Lancelot* and, whilst they were loading, I played a few tunes for his crew on the stern. The landing-craft was just about to move off when an air raid warning was sounded. Once that was over we motored across the bay towards our goal.

'Why don't you get on the bridge roof with your fiddle and give the ships a tune as we go past?' said the Cox'n.

'No thanks, I want to stay in the Navy.'

'Tell you what: if you play, I'll hoist a skull and crossbones.'

'Done!'

That's pretty safe, thought I; he's never got one of those. But pulling a Jolly Roger from his 'you-can't-see-me' suit, the Colour-Sergeant then hoisted it to the mast-head. Up to the bridge roof went the fiddler, with a can of beer to keep the fingers lubricated, and through the flotilla proceeded the LCU, with jigs and reels radiating all about. Guns' crews, look-outs and people generally showed their enthusiasm by cheers and applause and even the odd few dance steps. Then ahead loomed *Fearless*, with lots of gold braid about her bridge.

'I think that I shall be either a Lieutenant-Commander or a Sub-Lieutenant in about five minutes,' called down the musician. 'Keep playing. They've seen you now, anyway. keep playing!' And for good measure the Cox'n sounded his klaxon just in case they hadn't.

The gold braid disappeared from the bridge, to reappear a moment later with cameras and shouts of encouragement. There it was again: that superb sense of humour and spirit that helped us all through the bad times. That's what made our people special.

Arrived at *Lancelot* and moved on board. I leapt away to *Funella*, one of the trawlers, to see Tex Marshall who is the Chief MW onboard [Chief Petty Officer Mine Warfare: the expert on minesweeping and mines (ours)]. My, but hasn't he got older. We reminisced and caught up. The Captain gave me a bottle of Grouse [a favoured whisky] to take away. In the evening we had a small party in the *Lancelot's* Wardroom.

13.6.82 Sunday
Slept in, after getting up for breakfast at 0900, until nigh on 1400. Very hot curry lunch. Dhobi in evening. Phil [LS(D) Phil Kearns] not well. Lads moving into new mess deck.

Film at 1830. Supper – succulent turkey. To bed early but up again for drinkies with the SAS. [They appeared on board late at night. We did not know what they had been doing, nor who they were – and we did not ask. But what a nice lot.]

14.6.82 Monday
0200 air raid on Stanley. They are extending themselves! Quiet morning. Diving survey on *Antelope* in afternoon. Can we salvage the screws? Advance seems to be going well. Argies retreating in disorder, it appears. Life

aboard *Sir L* is quite pleasant. Good food, comfort and back to a feeling of detachment from it all.

1355. On board *Fearless*. 'The white flag is flying over Stanley.' *Ilhamdulillah*! Party tonight. However, stand by for air attack here? Brief in F followed by visit to Red Beach. Saw the Cpl Chef [Royal Marine Lenny Karnell] and the CPs. Failed to get a Parka [very warm anorak]. Back to *Sir L* for beer and chat with Purser [RFA supply officer] and a small kip.

During the evening the news came that both East and West Falkland had surrendered. Sent Shipgram to Fiddler:- 'Stanley Night. We're having a party. Request you write tune title "White Flag Over Stanley"! Team A1 this time. This is where the story really starts. Joke time now 1450. Bernie.'

And we had a party, did we ever. Sketches, songs, fiddle going well. A good one, mate! Finished around 0100 when an 'Awkward' warning came in. Slept well.

15.6.82 Tuesday
The WAR IS OVER. (official). How about that! However, we are still closed up at Air defence stations for who knows what might come over from Argy.

15,000 prisoners. Their CO asked for tentage for them and was told that it was in *Atlantic Conveyor* – which they sunk. Tough! A quiet day really. 2 hours Fiddle Practice in the Tank Deck Control Room. Cold but useful.

This evening, with the SBS and SAS newly arrived back on board, there were parties. One guy I met was Fred/George the SASer that I last met in Oman. Was called George then, now called Fred. [Wrong! Different guy, and it was Jim anyway – or was it?] Fiddle much in demand this evening and I played down the SAS/SBS mess below ours. Very rowdy. Later went down the Lads, mess for Piggy's birthday run. One thing that happened was a collection for one SBS Officer who was killed recently. They have the sextant he liberated from an Argy ship for his wife. Some notes large and small were thrown in from the Team. But despite the sadness (and 'laments' were going down well) it was good parties.

ON ISSUE WAR STOCK

Slashed survival suits
Survived as slashed suits, not as
'Suits (Slash) Survival';
But a slashed Suit (Survival)
As a survival suit (slashed)
Survives suitably
To splash below parachutes.

3

A Busy Peace

16.6.82 Wednesday
It has started. I dreamed that we were at a tented medical centre above the valley. An air attack came in and one could hardly see for flying debris. The white sweater I was wearing caught fire in the middle of a prolonged cannon attack. Taff Hurley lost the lower half of his left leg and was taken back to the shambles of the 'op' tent for treatment. His leg was left outside. Not a nice dream.

Very windy. Piggy away to *Baltic Ferry* [one of the 'STUFT' ships] to do a bottom search not done by Team 1 the other night. Meanwhile I took a small team to Blue Beach by Rigid Raider to clear one of the workboats screw. However, the thumping going into wind was such that one of the silly plastic quick-release buckles on the 'improved' version of the Clearance Divers Breathing Apparatus parted and we had to return for a new 'set' [underwater breathing set]. Recommended that W3 [Work boat No. 3] be towed back and hoisted. End of job. One of the Geminis broke adrift to the beach but we recovered it plus engine. Another late sesh this eve; ended up with the lads for an 'uckers' tournament in the Rec space [game similar to ludo, much loved by the Navy].

17.6.82 Thursday
Piggy away on *Antelope* after lunch to check screws, clearance above and remove port deck plate. I went to

Green Beach to visit Uncle Stan and Auntie Vi [related to Lieutenant-Commander R. Edwards, helicopter pilot, who had managed to get himself seconded to Special Forces as Liaison Officer]. He got his squeeze box out and I my fiddle. Unfortunately his tuned to C so no play together. [There are limits to one's ability: mine are the keys of G, D, and A.] But I gave them a few tunes. Green Beach is very pretty though it seems odd to see so many sangars [bunkers of local material used for shelter during air raids or as defensive positions], war equipment, helos and A/C in such a Scottish looking village. The Kelpers are very shy/quiet and after a bit I felt it better to leave. We had arrived by Gemini (Chas, Weir, myself and 4 SAS getting a lift) and we got a lift back in one of the LCUs from *Intrepid* (Colin Garwood's). Before lunch the *Cardiff* came alongside to give us water. The Padre came on board and we gave him a beer, or 3. *Cardiff* is looking quite war-weary and badly in need of paint/clean etc. Hot movie in evening – e.g. no ventilation. Sat up with the lads until late.

18.6.82. Friday
Quick trip to Red Beach before lunch. All moving out. Said goodbye to Teapot who wrote 'dit' for Fids in other book [Note book: quite a few people wrote 'dits' to Fiddler in it]. After lunch *Sir L* went to *Intrepid* to take on water and thereafter on a scenic tour of the sound before re-anchoring. Piggy away on *Antelope*. Returned late with Blondie Limerick and another CPO(D) in tow. Gave No 2 supper. Blondie reminiscing with SAS down their mess. I crashed out early but later asked to and did play down SAS mess. Crashed out around 0100. (Oh, we did watch a video in the evening. *Clash of Titans* – not the best.)

19.6.82 Saturday
Team out in the early hours looking at HMSM *Onyx* who had run into a pinnacle at 9 kts. Quite some

damage and both bow doors on one side stove in. Not a lot we can do though.

Piggy and Tommo away to Stanley. Dave plus 1 to Red and Blue Beach. Now, however, everything tight and no rabbits ['gizzits', as in 'That's nice, gizzit here'] going. Fuelled over at Blue Rover. In the evening Martin 'Biff' Davies (ex *Gavington*, Scotland RN Light-Heavyweight Champ) turned up from FCDT 2 in *Stena Seaspread* with some other Leading Divers. Nice to see him again and we had half an hour of reminiscing. Later, during the movie, everything turned sour. One of the visitors was reported to be found rummaging in SAS gear. They did not want to press charges. Left it to me. I put him under open arrest. An hour later Piggy had returned and walked straight into a situation where 3 of them had been caught looting a Starlight-sight (£1500). Returned to *Stena S* under custody. SAS very upset and crying for blood. Managed to assert Naval Discipline Act. Leaving it until John Dadd (Boss FCDT 2) [Warrant Officer Diver in charge of FCDT 2 on board *Stena Seaspread*] comes over tomorrow. But they are lucky to have survived the SAS. My lads are not happy, in fact downright embarrassed, as it was they who invited the culprits over. I am also not happy.

20.6.82 Sunday
John Dadd and Blondie Limerick over at first light. Chat, brief, meeting with SAS Major. Statements. Left. Apart from that it was a very quiet, boring Sunday.

Late this eve/night the SAS, or some of them, seemed to be fighting their own war in the messdeck.

RED BEACH

Aye mate, this is Falkland. Find a sangar over there. Bain't no demarkation: put your kit down anywhere. Always keep your weapon handy for the Argies flying low;

Air raids Red and Yellow any time – you never know.
That's the Navy Divers' castle (called Fort
Thompson): they're all mad,
Though the first to carry in the wounded from the pad.
There's a little extra water, seldom any half-way hot;
Medics take what's needed, we can have the stuff
that's not.
Them as crouching in the compound, Argy prisoners,
young and cowed,
Live on 'rat-pack' sundries from the half that we're
allowed.
That's a hole made by a bomb that bounced right here
upon the track.
Inside two more fester, stopping us from moving back.
Yeah, that frigate's always waiting close inshore like
that each day
Since they bombed us, so's to keep the Argy planes
away.
Oh, to get there for a dhobi or perhaps a beer or two!
Well, it's all yours, matey. Keep your head down!

Aye – and you!

21.6.82 Monday
To *Fearless* after lunch with Piggy for brief on next jobs and own input. Now are on standby for 2 × UXBs at Dunnose Head and the sinking of *Sir G* as a war grave.

How do you sink a tough old girl like *Galahad*? This is what I had been asked to do, and was the problem I now addressed. The trouble is that these ships have so many tanks and double bottoms that they are like honeycombs and very difficult to sink.

The hold of the ship, the only access to these compartments, was a total write-off, and there was no chance of getting the manhole covers off. Plan B, therefore, was to explode a line-charge along one water-line, capsize her and then blow the remaining tanks from outside.

Pointing out to the Staff that this would result in a long job and probably bodies floating about in the water, I suggested that perhaps a couple of the Navy's newest torpedoes would do the job in short order. This suggestion was not looked upon with favour at the time, but it was later adopted as the best solution.

We never did get to go back on board and glad we were of it. No one likes to kill a ship, particularly one with whom so much had been shared.

Also have job to test extent of mine/bomb burial in San Carlos waters [to see how deep they have sunk into the silt and consequently determine the problems involved in destroying them]. Stopped off at *Stena Seaspread* on the way back to give the RN Captain a feel for this looting case aboard and our view. This he required, according to the RPO [Regulating Petty Officer of the Naval party on board]. Not welcomed, although allowed a seat. Not interested and came away without a farewell and a flea in my ear. The man is not even polite. Pissed off with that Regulator giving me duff gen. [I never really understood this. His lads had fouled up, not mine, so why all this palaver? perhaps a sort of defensive position – but why?]

Back on board we heard of the Princess of Wales's baby and after an initial on-board apathy, got a party going and the rum and fiddle out. Other parties around too but I stayed in the Wardroom one. The toast of the day was:

'To the Heir to the Heir to the Throne.'

22.6.82 Tuesday

The 'Splicers' signal ['Splice the main brace'; a signal for the Navy to indulge in a little celebratory rum] came in today for Navy and RFA. Everyone a bit late in getting up after last night's parties. Ship moved to new anchorage with *Stena Seaspread* [used as a heavy repair ship and invaluable to the task force] alongside. This followed by the Lads having their tot and Queens of grog [Queen's: the name given to any rum left over from an issue; grog: rum mixed with water]. Only RN, RM and RCT allowed. We had our own little ceremony behind closed doors and most people went round for Queens twice. Bottled and sealed the last of my Navy Neaters and labelled it 'SAN CARLOS WATER'. I will give it to Harry for his, Fiddler's and my consumption later.

As we left the Swan Hotel at Devonport on the start of this Great Adventure, Harry Hartop the publican had given me a bottle filled with some of the Royal Navy rum that had been discontinued so long ago. The stocks left with the RN had been sold off in the early seventies and this was about the last of it in Harry's private cellar. Determined to save it for some special occasion, I had been at great pains to keep it as safe as my fiddle. Now that the signal to splice the main brace had been received, this seemed the appropriate moment to broach this special gift.

The Team assembled and each man had his tot. It is pretty potent stuff, is 'pusser's rum', and none of the commercial brands, except Hick's Special Reserve, seem to have the attack potential of the original. In consequence there were many watery eyes on this occasion, some from nostalgia but most from the unexpected effects of its imbibition.

With 50 per cent thus properly disposed of, the decision was made to decant the remainder into a half-bottle, cork and seal it, and hope to return it to the Swan Hotel for a suitable celebration there in due time. Perhaps then we could share a small piece of the whole adventure together.

At 'Splicers' I was asked to give the toast, which I did as yesterday. Very few saw it off properly. [Traditionally it should be drunk in one swallow.] After, we had braised Upland Goose, courtesy of Lt Cdr Roger Edwards, who seems to be related to everyone on Falkland.

As officers and seniors gathered together in the saloon prior to the evening meal, there was an air of festivity about, a feeling of a job well done and satisfaction at the outcome. Add to this the 'splicers' signal, and the scene was ripe for a party.

Roger Edwards, who had spent the last few days visiting various relatives around the Islands as part of his liaison duties, had collected all sorts of goodies from them. Now, as dinner was announced, he banged with his fist on the deck-head and called out, 'Gentlemen: tonight, courtesy of the Kelpers, for every man in the ship – roast upland goose!'

Cheers and applause.

'And,' cried a particularly well-groomed and thoroughly charming Special Forces officer, 'a bottle of wine to every table!'

More cheers; then a voice, 'But there isn't any.'

The officer continued, 'No, two bottles of Chablis to each table!'

'But where are you going to get it? We drank the last of the wine weeks ago.'

'My dear fellow,' rejoined our friend, 'first thing I packed. I've got two cases of it down below.'

A year later we met up again in the killing-house at Hereford, and I asked him about this. He confided that he had had 'the devil's own job' keeping the stuff with his kit but was determined that, when the time came, it would be available to mark a suitable occasion.

Between Harry and him, they certainly had the thing right. A little style goes a long, long way and this bit of style had come six thousand miles or more.

Later in the evening I went down to the Lads' mess for a couple of cans. A small party until about 0300 or 0400. At some stage later the fire alarm started and everyone to emergency stations. Someone had let off a smoke canister in the hangar.

23.6.82 Wednesday
Woken by L/S Davies telling me to 'leap across' and see the RN Captain. So I got up etc and went to *Stena* – negative Capt. Doing defaulters! So wait. Waited an hour and then he called me in to complain about the state of our Ship and the unlimited 'boozing' going on. I think he should have been talking to *Lancelot*'s Chief Officer. Obviously bad staff work on his part. After a clipped 'Sir!' I left. Wazzik! found out later that he has been getting up everyone's noses and is generally considered a no-no; not that he'll be worried.

Got a signal saying 'Move to Stanley half the team.' Eventually got away, with personal kit only, to *Intrepid* at 1630. Piggy and I plus 8. But why no gear?

On board *Intrepid* and down 4M1 mess. Taken up to the Sgt's Mess and played fiddle as promised. Quick sleep then watched a movie. Left at dusk for Stanley. In the evening, after dinner, played for the wardroom which was much appreciated it seems. Especially the 'eighteen consecutive notes all the same' in 'Life on the Ocean Wave' [The only regimental or corps march with this distinction]. Then a wet in the Sgt's Mess before turning in for a very hot/uncomfortable night.

Change time zone to Q.

24.6.82 Thursday
Mick Fellows plus Fleet Team 1 arrived on board to collect kit. Mick took me back to Stanley with him. What a wonderful trip; in to Stanley water through the narrows and there was a very pretty and colourful town ahead of us.

Everything seems so much smaller than I imagined. Ancient hulks are used as storage and we have part of one for our store. We took a walk through the high street and found Post Office, QHM [Queen's Harbour Master] etc. Mud everywhere but they are cleaning up. Everyone seems to be moving out. Chris Meatyard was on board *Sir B* when we got aboard. [RFA *Sir Bedivere* moored alongside the main jetty and used as HQ accommodation ship]. Piggy having difficulty following from *Intrepid*. Chris and I went off to Gov't House which is also HQ. Got me on a Wasp helo [small helicopter used for anti-submarine attacks from frigates; we walked across to it, got in and the pilot inserted the ignition key, started up, checked his mirror and away we flew – much like a car, really] and away across land to San Carlos and *Sir L*. Surprised the boys but got 3 sets of diving suits away and back to Stanley. Grabbed a sandwich, which I ate in the plane [helo]. Noticed shell holes in the peat around the Argy defences by Twin Sisters etc.

Back aboard, *Sir B*, Piggy plus Team arrived. Late lunch. Read mail. Letters from Ma and Fiddler also from Gareth (next door) and two cards from Margarette. Took fiddle for a walk to The Rose Pub. No one at home but met Heather Pederson [relation of Roger Edwards and wife of Tony the well-known Bisley shot] and played for her family in their kitchen. Back aboard had a bath and dhobi, a couple of beers, supper and then a video before bed. Mess full of lots of high ranking officers. General Moore there plus the Commodore Amphibious Warfare. Did not stop there long. Mess full of Officers (sleeping mess, that is).

25.6.82 Friday
An interesting day. Helo'd out to *Cordella* sweeping in the minefields. Then to *Junella* who was disposal ship. [She followed behind the others, sinking swept mines by gunfire.] Weather force 5 and rising. Second mine swept was for recovery. Tex Marshall (Ch MW), Buffer [Senior Leading Seaman (MW) on board] and I went away to it. Buffer bumped it. I bailed out and did an inspection. Managed to roll it over so Tex could see underside. Looked like the classic 7 horn (Hertz) German mine. Attached 2-pennant strop [modified Gemini sling] to the two lifting lugs and eventually got it to *Junella*, by this

time in unswept waters! Tow passed and we went off towards Fitzroy. On arrival, mine taken by 2 × Gemini in tow 3 miles up the creek while *Junella* anchored. Mine then anchored and marked. Talking to Chris Meatyard by radio, on arrival back at ship, found mine to be same as German GY but smaller. Is this a new mine? Looks like it. Now we wait for team to arrive tomorrow so I can dive on it for an 'ID' [identification].

Winching down from a helo on to the bridge-deck of a wildly rolling and pitching trawler is an experience that would set anyone's heart racing. Apart from the fact that the deck is rising and falling at an alarming rate, even in the middle of the ship, there are other, nastier things trying to get you. As the ship plunges about, the mast and derricks describe great arcs in the air and attempt to bludgeon the descending man when he is not looking. Attached to these aerial coshes are guys and stays of taut wire rope that endeavour to trap and tear at a fellow too. There is not a great deal that you can do about all this, except fend off as best you can and put your trust in pilot and winchman. As they are Fleet Air Arm, you can be pretty certain that, however many goes it takes, you will be set down in one piece; for they are the world's experts at this sort of thing.

Shortly after our arrival in *Cordella*, the second mine of the day was swept. There followed a discussion with the Command (Lieutenant-Commander Martin Holloway) as to what it was and what we should do with it. None of the clearance divers could positively identify it as something we knew, though it did bear a resemblance to one of the German horned mines of the Second World War. The mine, or one like it, needed to be recovered, since no one knew just what kind of weapon this was. The weather was deteriorating, and the general opinion of the Command was that live-mine recovery in those conditions was not on, and perhaps the next one swept in better weather would do just as well.

> The decision to recover a drifting mine by towing it ashore should not be made lightly . . . it may be possible to secure a hemp hawser to a lifting strop or eyebolt but this should be attempted only under ideal weather conditions . . . a decision to use render-safe procedures may be made only if the mine can be positively identified.
>
> *Extracted from contemporary RN publications*

I argued that a mine on the surface is worth any number still submerged, so sense prevailed and the capture was on. Borrowing a woolly bear and a rubber bag (acrylic pile long johns and a diving suit of rubberised canvas), I proceeded to the stern for transfer to the mine disposal ship, *Junella*, that was following along behind. If my arrival had been somewhat spectacular, then so was my departure, although these boys did it every day. The Gemini was allowed to slide stern-first down the net recovery ramp aft, and then checked before hitting the water. With the crew inboard (in the Gemini) the signal was given to let go, and the boat fell off the ramp and was left floating in the wash as the ship continued on her way. The engine started first time and round we swung, bouncing over the waves towards *Junella*. Only seeing our destination on each wave crest, we approached from aft. The Gemini was driven boldly up the ramp as far as it would go, hooked on to the winch and hauled up to the deck. What a way to arrive! – splendid seamanship coupled with confidence and daring.

Once on board, having made my number with the Captain, my old friend Mark Rowledge, and explained the situation, I met up again with Tex, the Mine Warfare Chief, and we set about working out how to capture our prey. We had noticed two eye-plates that showed from time to time as the seven-tenths submerged mine wallowed in the foam-streaked sea.

A Gemini lifting pennant of wire rope was lashed into three legs and made ready in the recovery boat.

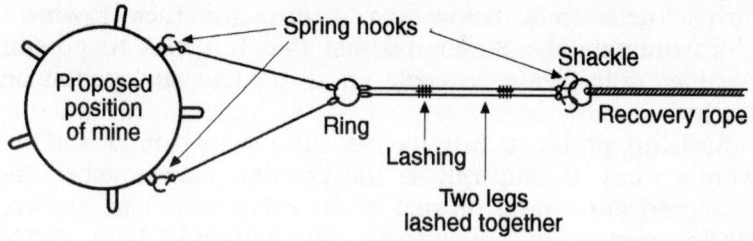

None of us had ever had occasion to snaffle a live mine before, so once again it was a question of minimum numbers. My job was to do the hands-on stuff, Tex was the recorder and recognition expert and Smudge, the Buffer (chief boatswain's mate), was cox'n of the rubber boat. Perhaps when we got a close look we would find that it was of a known 'brand' and we would not have to recover it after all. *Junella* could then sink it by gun-fire and we could all go home.

We launched and rode, getting visual indications from 'mother' on the crest of each wave. Having reached the mine, we proceeded to circle it. There was nothing to see that we had not already noted by binocular from the ship's bridge, so now we would have to look underneath.

This particular type of mine is actuated by a ship hitting it and bending one of the soft lead horns. Inside, a glass vial of electrolite then fractures, the liquid runs into a waiting battery, and an instant electrical charge is shot to the detonator which, thus encouraged, does its business with the primer and explodes the main charge. This blows a ruddy great hole in the ship which then sinks. This much we could tell without difficulty. Consequently it was important not to bump or hang on to these convenient though lethal 'handholds'. We did not know how many horns there were below the water, nor their position. Unfortunately the Buffer did just that but, the boat being flexible, didn't initiate such an ultimately dire sequence. Lucky!

Still, no problem: just have a little swim round and see what's what. Bailing out of the Gemini, I approached the mine and got a hold on one of the eye-plates. This allowed me to orientate myself towards the mine and I then started to investigate the underwater surface by feel, something at which we clearance divers are most adept. While I was carrying out this initial inspection, a larger wave with a breaking top advanced unseen upon the situation, and suddenly I was in a welter of foam and thrown heavily against the device. My shoulder came hard into contact with one of the lead horns – which bent. I pushed off, and Tex said later that it looked like someone playing with a large beach-ball in the surf.

Swimming back and grappling with the weapon once again, I managed to roll it over and expose the bottom plate and mooring lever to Tex's scrutiny. The action clinched the matter since, although it resembled the classic German mine, this one proved to be something entirely new to us, and it would have to be taken apart.

I swam with the towing pennant to the mine and clipped the spring hooks on to the eye-plates. Everything fitted nicely and I swam back to the boat. Now began the dodgy bit, towing it back to the ship. If the waves turned the mine and the wire pennant bent a horn, we were not far enough away in our little boat to escape the subsequent blast. No matter, plug on! Somehow we did not seem to be getting any nearer to the mother ship. We were making slow and uncomfortable progress, climbing up one sea and racing down the other side, before coming up all-standing as the tow-rope jerked taut. Eventually *Junella* came to us. We bent a lengthy hawser on to our tow-rope, slipped off and were recovered up the ramp.

On the bridge, as we started the long haul into Fitzroy Sound with the mine following along behind, I asked Mark

TOMMO'S 'BAD' PHOTO – while waiting to be lifted off *Tristram* by helo, we decided to 'look the part' in order to discourage anyone else from stealing our gear.

TEAM WAITING TO MOVE – With everything packed up and ready to go, the Team waits for Colin Garwood's landing craft to arrive. Left to right: Whiskey, Wheels, Taff R. and Rex. John Boy sitting in front of Buster, then Taff H. and Jock R. behind Joe. Standing are: Phil, BB, Chas and Dave.

FIDDLER IN THE FLEET – The stern deck of Col. Sgt. Garwood's LCU (Colin in beret) with BB about to start the impromptu concert that lifted Fleet morale after another San Carlos air raid.

'THE GLEANER' – Once again John Lawyer has captured the essence of the action as the diver approaches the erratically rolling mine, spring hook in hand, and judges his moment to swim forward and slip on before the next wave races upon him.

TOMMO AND THE MINE – You can just tell how cold the water was in Fitzroy Sound.

Lifting the mine over the sandbar.

BB checking the fit of the *Junella* sledge and the base-plate and mooring spindle.

The mine on its sledge just clear of high water and still with some yards to go.

TOMMO – Ever by my side, Tommo was in truth my right-hand man. We shared a rapport seldom found between two people, born out of adversity and mutual respect. Note: the single neoprene glove he is wearing is half of the only pair we had.

TOMMO MEETS THE MEAN MAD MINE ONCE MORE – Some months later, when the mine had been returned to the UK, Tommo was invited to join the team of divers responsible for steaming the explosives out of the mine-case. This messy, sick-making task was the final act in the drama that rendered the device quite safe and suitable for display.

PLAYING OUT *FALKLAND SOUND*'S CAPTAIN (See entry 2.7.82) – Although not appreciated by one senior officer, the lads of the crew are obviously enjoying the occasion.

IN THE VICTORY BAR – Tommo, John Boy and Jock I (behind him: Phil, Buster and Charlie).

PIGGY AND HIS FAMOUS DUFFLE-COAT WITH BB (on the jetty outside the FCDT 3 'office')

GOING – after the SAS party, waiting to board the Herky-bird. Who were those masked men?

IN HERCULES No. 206 ON THE WAY TO ASCENSION – Finally, the tension released, the men of the FCDT 3 'crashed out' wherever they could. With no space to stretch out, BB plays fiddle at 20,000ft. No-one could hear anyway, there was far too much noise.

BB BACK HOME AND DOWN THE PUB – Good ale, good friends, good music – what more could any man need?

how it was he had taken so long to get to us. He pointed out that we had drifted into unswept waters and, when it became apparent that we were not going to be able to tow the mine out against the wind and sea, he had stood-to, closed down and had come to collect us. A courageous decision and typical of the man.

Arriving at Fitzroy, *Junella* went in as far as she could, cast the mine adrift and anchored. As dusk was falling we took two Geminis on parallel tow lines (long ones) and pulled the 'beast' a mile or so into calm and shallower water. Here we anchored it for the night, lit by a battery of flashing beacon lights. We did not want anyone to bump into it, not after all the trouble we had taken to capture it.

26.6.82 Saturday
Weather still bad. Waited until midday for Piggy and Tommo to arrive. No sign. Helo trouble. So Tex, Buffer and I went to do the mine inspection. Moored close and while I rolled it about, we measured, checked and described while Tex wrote and drew. Back on board we drew a fair sketch of it, finishing just before Tommo plus Piggy arrived. Looking in CBs [specialist publications indispensable to the Team] we found nothing like it. We've got a new one, folks! P, T and I went for a further inspection, this time Tommo in the water. Back aboard thought, discussed, ate and talked to Chris M on radio. He was away in another world but we eventually got some sense out of him. Beach it tomorrow then go collect another in case the first blows. Watched dreadful movie while Tex and Tommo made up the *Junella* Sledge [improvised equipment designed to ease the transition of the mine from water to land without destroying it] to beach the brute tomorrow. Wrote to Fids, Ma and Dick. This is the Big One!

HMS *Junella*
At Bluff Cove
26th June 82

Yer Fiddler,

Three of us are detached from the Team at present and down here to do the BIG ONE. We have managed to capture an Argy Mine and tomorrow start the job of taking it to pieces. I think this is probably the first one captured for some time, possibly since Korea. Tomorrow we beach it on the tide before going out to collect another one. We want a second one in case the first blows. This is a new type of Mine and we know nothing about it despite having all the books with us. No one has ever seen one before. Today we gave it a close inspection in choppy waters. This was easy compared with getting it yesterday. I had to hook on a towing bridle in breaking seas which rather tumbled it and me about a bit. However, we eventually managed to get it in here and safely anchored. So the next few days will be quite interesting.

I could not tell you before as it was delicate information (and even now you should keep the contents of this letter under wraps) but we managed to remove two live 1000 lb bombs out of two LSLs (*Sir Galahad* and *Sir Lancelot*) during the air attacks in Bomb Alley. The jobs took eight-and-a-half and twenty-two-and-a-half hrs respectively. I am so pleased with the way the boys worked. As I put in my report, 'In the highest traditions of the Service'. And you should have seen them on Red Beach. They have earned the highest praise from several senior officers, not only for their diving and B+MD work but as stretcher bearers, hospital orderlies, diggers, builders and every job going. As the Colonel of the Beach said to me one particularly bad night, 'Yours are the scruffiest Sailors I have ever seen, but they make wonderful nurses and thank God they're here.'

I leave you with an anon poem I found pinned up in the CP:-

It's a cold wind, the West Wind full of Argies' cries.
I never hear the West Wind for the hand in front of mine eyes.
It comes from Port Stanley, Twin Sisters too.
Death is in the West Wind – and Victory too.

That's it, Dad.
  'Keep your head down.'
  See you soon – *inshallah*.

                Bernie

                            Saturday, 26th June

Dear Ma,

So, here we are in the Falklands at last and THE WAR IS OVER. Now starts the clearing-up and we have been allocated a small job down in the Fitzroy area. We did manage to get here a little time ago, while things were still rather hot, but there was little I could say just then. However, we had some interesting things to do at the time, which kept us quite busy. Some of the challenges we were given stretched us rather a lot but the boys behaved magnificently and I am VERY proud of them. They did everything that was asked of them and then more. There were no complaints, no dissent – just pure enthusiasm and dedicated expertise, as one would expect from Clearance Divers. They are, after all, the cream of the Navy. My second in command, Chief Trotter, has been a gallant bastion of support. One particular diver, Tommo Thompson, has been at my right hand in all our enterprises so far. I could not have wished for a better companion.

    I do not have the time to write much more now as there is still this last job to do. Suffice it to say that it has been a great adventure that I would not have missed for anything.

If I never do anything else again, ever, this has to be the apogee of life.

Now that it is all over, I cannot see them keeping us here much longer; so I will tell you all about it when I come home.

Soon,
All my love,
Nigel

APOGEE

Sing no sad songs for me
If I come second in tomorrow's race;
The opposition, mine to leave,
Could, with deception,
All my skill outpace.

Play no lament for me
If I misread the signals of the game;
The steadiness I must achieve
Should, with attainment,
Stay the waiting flame.

Shed no soft tears for me
If I am vanquished in the coming bout;
The uppercut I might receive
Would far surpass the
Ultimate knockout.

27.6.82 Sunday
Set off with most of the MWs [Mine Warfare Ratings] in 3 Geminis to beach the mine. Tommo and I did the beach recce and then swam the mine in and, with some difficulty, put it on the *Junella* Sledge. With the use of some planks and a bit of 'umph' [a very, very long piece of rope with every available person pulling on it] we got the whole thing on to the shore and then returned to the

ship. After a period of waiting we got hold of Meatyard on the wireless and approval to go ahead with the RSP [Render Safe Procedure]. We were warned to be careful as Intelligence believed it to be topped up with anti-stripping devices. Cheers!

Tex, Piggy, Tommo and I left for the beach. It took us two hours to render it safe. Started by removing the base/mechanism plate, by unscrewing and blowing the last two (nuts). An expert bit of demolition by Piggy. Found the actuation method and what was either a detonator or primer-placer. The wires went somewhere else. [This caused some puzzlement.] Then took off the top plate nut and plate itself by hammer and chisel and remotely by improvised method. The top plate of the primer tube removed but primers fast in there. Removed the filler plate at the bottom but no go there either. Turned my attention to the det/primer-placer (previously moved out) and found that by moving the tube forward, what turned out to be the 'det' could be removed. End of RSP.

Tex gave good interpretation of the workings and Tommo was an excellent back up. We then put it back together, sealed the base plate and 'umphed' it [just the four of us this time] back to the water. 1½ hrs tow back to the ship where it was winched on board. We had a good meal and while the ship moved to Berkley Sound watched the film *Apocalypse Now*, much to Tommo's enjoyment. Martin Holloway, MCM 11 [officer in charge of the 11th Mine Countermeasures Squadron (the trawlers)] , came on board, envious and congratulatory.

It was an interesting job doing that mine. A proper, if improvised, RSP was worked out and signalled to the others at long range. Everything worked well but it was discovered that if the mines are left for a long time and marine growth clogs the mooring spindle, even if it is swept, it will remain live for ever. Dangerous! We were lucky.

The time had come to beach the mine, and Tommo and I went ahead of the other two Geminis to find a convenient strand suitable to our needs. We explored the shore and a couple of creeks but everywhere there was thick kelp lying off shore. This would prevent a successful beaching operation. In one creek, sitting atop an emplacement used by the guns bombarding Stanley defences, there was an enormous eagle. He did not seem concerned by the sound of the engine, nor by our greetings to him, and it occurred to us that he might have been deafened by the guns. As we came close he spread his huge wings and languidly flapped away. Perhaps after all he had seen so much that two men in a Gemini were not really worth bothering about.

Shifting further along the shore, we came across a low, sandy headland protected by an offshore sand-bar. There was no kelp and it seemed to be a good place for a mine-beaching. Our recce proved that this was indeed the perfect spot, even to the disused sangar a short way up the slope that could be used as a bunker.

Piggy, Tex and the ship's Mine Warfare Ratings arrived with the *Junella* Sledge and the mine in tow. The Sledge was taken inshore and the MWs laid out their longest hawser inland from it. The next, rather more difficult phase was to walk the mine over the sand-bar and seat it upon the Sledge. Piggy stayed to seaward with a couple of companions in one Gemini and all the rest retired inland. Tommo and I slipped into the freezing water and headed for the sullenly floating mine.

We had but one pair of neoprene gloves between us and these we shared, each wearing a glove on the hand that would grasp the underwater projections of the 'beast'. The two of us were either side of the mine as we slowly guided it shorewards until our feet touched bottom. Close to the sand-bar the water became quite shallow, and the mine had to be gently but firmly lifted to clear the bottom. This took a little time since it weighed some hundreds of pounds and must not be allowed to roll and damage a horn.

Suddenly there came a shout from Piggy: 'Leopard seal!'

Of all the creatures in these waters, this was the one to fear. The seal family's answer to the shark, it would ferociously attack anything that swam. Looking out to sea, we saw a huge, black creature bearing down upon us with its head and shoulders well above the surface and its moustache bristling. It came at such speed that it produced a bow wave and a wash; but there is not much you can do about that when you are balancing a mine in waist-deep water. It dived and we waited, expecting at any moment to be violently assaulted and scanning the water in an effort to see from where it would come. Minutes passed as we continued shorewards, but the creature did not reappear.

Having managed by main force to half lift, half float the mine over the sand-bank, we reached the slightly deeper waters beyond and the waiting *Junella* Sledge. This had been ballasted with divers' weight-belts, but even so we had to stand upon it to ease the great green sphere into its place. Once we had it secured, the signal was given to Piggy, now ashore, to start the heave. The men were a good way away and the hawser was heavy but, with the aid of planks on the soft sand and with Tommo and me steadying, they managed to drag the Sledge and its cargo up above the high-water mark. As Piggy said at the time,

'I hope the RAF EOD boys don't come along. They will see it above the high-water mark and claim it as theirs.'

So we left it there for the time being and returned to the ship to make final preparations for the Render Safe Procedure (RSP).

In order to render safe mines and bombs, the Royal Navy equips its Clearance Diving Teams with all sorts of splendid, if old-fashioned, doohickeys and gilguys. There are devices for X-raying metal to see the inner workings of a weapon. There is a wonderful non-magnetic tool kit, full of grabbers, twisters, wrenchers, prisers, pullers and lifters, packed in five large boxes, that is capable of dealing with any situation. There are lights, cameras and far-lookers, remote control robots, blocks, pulleys, stakes and cordage, as well as a host of other gear. None of this did we have.

It had been considered in the UK that we would have no need of it. I was not happy about the fact then, and I was no happier as we prepared to take this mine apart.

All officers and senior rates in the Branch are trained in the delicate task of obtaining access to and removing fuses and detonators; but what we had all seen in films and on television, the man crouched beside the weapon carefully removing its component parts by hand, does not happen any more. Remote RSP (Render Safe Procedure) is the name of the game and that was what we were about this time. Unfortunately, having none of the proper kit, it was a question of using what was to hand. One thing we knew from inspecting our quarry was that it was neither magnetic nor acoustic, so we could use ordinary tools at a pinch. However, we had been told that in all probability it was equipped with anti-stripping devices or booby traps; those amusing little extras that the enemy fits to take out the operator by arranging for the mine to detonate at an inopportune moment. We believed that these would be either light-sensitive or fitted into the circuitry or mechanism – probably the latter. An interesting problem to solve.

We worked out in advance exactly what steps would be taken. Each one would be signalled to the sangar at start and finish so that, if something went wrong and the mine detonated, the back-up team would know what _not_ to do next time. Piggy, Tex and Tommo then retired to the bunker and the RSP was started. At the end of each set of actions an inspection was undertaken and the next set worked out. It was a long but fascinating game to play.

Elsewhere in this narrative there is an account of the technical proceedings. Suffice it to say that, using a hammer, a padded chisel, an adjustable spanner, a bag of explosives and a very long piece of 'string' for remote control, we eventually reached the stage where there was but one course of action left to us. We could see a brass cylinder with a wing-nut and two ball-catches on it, but could not see a connection to the electrical circuitry. It was clear that here was either the detonator or a sliding primer that fitted around a hidden initiator. Either way it had to come out. There was no chance, deep inside the casing as it was, that we would be able to remove it remotely. It would have to be taken out by hand. But which way to turn it?

Could this be the classic anti-stripping device?

There was no way to determine either answer except by doing it.

We had to know how these things worked because our ships were still out there looking for them.

There was no time to waste and dusk was approaching.

We four had a final chat together and then went our separate ways: three to the bunker, one to the beach.

Back to the problem.
Undo the retaining wing-nut.
Done.
Push the cylinder in and up.
Yes.
Then, should it be turned clockwise or anti-clockwise?
Think. Decide.
One way – it might detonate.
The other – it might not.
But which way to go?
Frozen into indecision
A last look round and then decide.

I remember, as in a photograph, that it was a peaceful evening. Looking south and west, the colours of the approaching dusk were quite beautiful over the low headlands and inlets of Fitzroy Sound. A single helicopter, a little north of the usual route, was steadily approaching. I suppose he must have noticed something on the beach for he veered towards us and came to a hover near by.

Now, if you are flying a chopper on a stores run, I should imagine that things can get a little monotonous and any unusual sight must be welcome; but when that sight is

121

a kneeling man with half his arm thrust inside a large, green, very obviously horned mine, and when you notice other men crouched low in a sangar nearby vigorously waving you away, it would not be surprising if you suddenly lost your curiosity. So, pulling full collective lift, the helo launched itself violently up and back from the hover and shot away south-eastwards.

The spell was broken.
Decision
Twist anti-clockwise – and – la voilà! One detonator removed.
One mine rendered safe. Phew!

Dusk was falling as we put the now harmless mine back together and manhandled it into the water. There followed a long cold haul back to the ship, and under the stern arc lights we transferred the tow to the lifting equipment in order to hoist the mine inboard. Piggy was fumbling with one hand under the weapon trying for an eye-plate, when into the light of the arcs swam, just below us, some pretty little dolphins with black and white markings much reminiscent of the . . .

'Killer whale!', Tommo and I shouted to Piggy, who took one look and snatched his hand inboard. Well, it repaid him for his 'Leopard seal!' It is always nice to end the day with a laugh. This jape broke the tension to which we had all been subject, and *Junella*'s ship's company must have wondered why the four of us were collapsed in the boat, helpless with mirth.

28.6.82 Monday
Junella sailed in bad weather before first light and spent most of the day acting as disposal ship for the rest in the lap. [Minesweeping is done in strips called 'laps'.] 99% of the task completed by the end of today. Piggy, Tommo and I spent most of the day asleep. Removed the horns off the mine for safety. Into Port Stanley in time to take

a walk round, visit QHM and Post Office. Visited the Pettersons with Piggy. A good welcome. Promised to fix their fiddle which was broken. Auntie Vi was there from Port San Carlos. Delighted to see me/her. Quick visit to see Auntie Velma at The Rose, but she was very busy and so did not stay. But one does not expect much from these people until they've had a chance to think about it for a day or two.

Back on board. Very crowded. Some mailies [letters]. Supper, video and bed in a much crowded mess. A bit hot really.

Jock Weir has shaved off his set – as has Whiskey Walker. Fined one crate of beer for doing so without permission. Taff Hurley's looking a little more ragged. Joe's still smiling, Wheels still writing to his wife, Taff Reece seems to be getting a bit more talkative. Chas sits and smiles. Charlie is as pixie-like as ever. Buster's looking older. Rex hasn't changed. Tommo's glad it's over, Phil's still in *Lancelot*; so is Jock Rebecca. John Boy retains his quizzical smile and Dave is slimmer and glad to be going home.

29.6.82 Tuesday
Wrote out the report on the Mine RSP this morn. Glad that's over. Copy in records. Delivered it to Chris Meatyard at COMAW's [Commodore Amphibious Warfare] and then returned via the Pettersons to fix Tony's fiddle. Restrung and rebridged it but the tail piece fractured on tuning. Shame. Gave them some tunes anyway before returned to *Sir B*. The lads have all the gear off *Sir L*. Did that at 0130. Today sorting. We have to send a team to Fitzroy to recover *Tristram*'s stern door.

He was a short man with bristly moustaches and an aggressive manner. I was chatting with *Bedivere* officers about the *Tristram* job when he strutted up and interrupted our discussion.

'So you're responsible!' he snorted.

'Hello, I'm Bernie,' seemed the polite thing to say, even if he was a Major.

'You're the one who blew the back door off Tristram!' He ignored any social niceties.

'Well, yes. I did do that job.'

'Where is it?' he demanded belligerently.

'Hanging under the stern, when I last saw it.'

'No, it's not. What have you done with it?'

He was beginning to get tiresome.

I patted my pockets, looked perplexed and told him, 'Well now, I had it when I came out . . . .'

He made snorting noises and went away. I wonder who he was. He did seem very agitated.

At about this time we received a fresh intake of naval officers from the UK, whose one concession to the situation seemed to be that they did not wear ties with their white shirts. FCDT 3 were still limited to the clothes we stood up in, and no prospect of any more yet awhile. Our dhobi routine was for the Team to take over the laundry and showers, put all our clothes into the machines, and hang around in the bathroom until they were done. Then, washed and in fresh warm kit once again, we would continue on our way.

My set of clothing consisted of sea-boots, two pairs of arctic socks, long johns, 'you-can't-see-me' trousers, vest, Norwegian polo-neck Army shirt, neckerchief (yellow, a gift from a mate), head-over, thick Skye sweater (dark blue) and 'you-can't-see-me' jacket. This was topped off by a naval beret, or flat hat when doing dodgy things, and a pair of white gymshoes for wearing in the Wardroom.

Many of the new arrivals objected loudly to our rig, but never thought to inquire as to the reason. One even went so far as to steal a clean pair of arctic socks from my bunk. They were very good at voicing comments like, 'Nice to see the lads saluting again,' and, 'About time we got rid of all these cowboys, if you ask me.' But then again, I expect they were feeling a bit left out of things.

WE ARE THE COWBOYS

We are the Cowboys;
I've heard you say it loudly in the bar,
Although well hidden by the smoke of your cigar.
We are the Cowboys,
Because our hair's too long
And uniform is wrong;
We are the Cowboys
In spite of our success
And 'coz of wearing gymshoes in the Mess.

We are the Cowboys;
It must be so, 'coz Staff are never wrong.
You do not know us, but we'll jolly you along.
We are the Cowboys,
A denigrating word
To make us seem absurd;
We are the Cowboys
Because we wear no rank
And hold that certain 'johnny-lates' are dank.

We are the Cowboys.
You think that sailors should be awed and cowed,
But we dare to be different – and that ain't allowed.
We are the Cowboys,
Because we are 'alive'
And that we Clearance Dive.
We are the Cowboys,
We have unique rapport
And talk with 'Super-Secrets' and the Corps.

We are the Cowboys,
And I suspect you'll quash us if you can;
You have the Admiral's ear, you are the Precious Man.
We are the Cowboys –
You make that very clear,

To anyone who'll hear.
We are the Cowboys
Because we look so 'bad',
But what do you know of the jobs we've had?

29th June 1982
Port Stanley

Yer Fiddler,

Well, we managed to sort out the mine OK and it will soon be on its way to the UK for the boffins to look at. Come to that, we shall be leaving Stanley on 7th July (*inshallah*) to fly back to UK. The wheres and whens are not known yet, we just look forward to getting back.

Fiddle is going well and it turns out that I am the only fiddler in the South Atlantic. As yet the only other musician I have met is another MCD who plays 'harps'. There is still a curfew, we are not allowed out after 5 p.m. local, and all the Pubs are closed. Hopefully though, we will get a 'wet' and a tune in one before we go.

The lads are in good heart and all together here now, back aboard *Sir Galahad*. [Of course this should read *Sir Bedivere*, but perhaps *Galahad* was still very much in our minds.] There seems to be an almost indecent haste for people to get themselves back to UK. We hear that the *Daily Mirror* has had Newcastle Breweries concoct a special ale for the Task Force and are sending it down to us here. At the rate things are going, the people who eventually get it will be those who replaced those for whom it was made in the first place.

But really, it is time to go home. The saluting has started again, especially among the Guards; and I saw a division of men being inspected – standing ankle deep in mud! I am OK as I wear combats, gymshoes, civi sweater, flat hat and yellow neckerchief and nobody knows who I am. No badges of rank visible but one handy for emergencies. In the Wardroom where the Staffies gather, we are beginning to hear comments like: 'Nice to see the men saluting again' and 'We really must start enforcing dress regulations' and 'About time we got rid of some of these "pirates".' Yes – it's time we came home and left the place to the peacetime soldiers/sailors. If they have another war they can give us a shout.

I am writing this on a copy of *Globe and Laurel* in the Officers' 'Dormitory' in *Sir Galahad* [*Sir Bedivere*]. You should have seen the looks on some of the Senior Staff Officers' faces during the switch-off party when I did the Cabaret and prefixed it with, 'Right, pay attention this way, keep silence, pin your ears back . . .'

So that's your lot, see yer soon (*inshallah*) when big silver bird drops us off somewhere in UK, or shortly after. Teapot should be back soon.

Bernie

30.6.82 Wednesday
The morning spent on a trip to the Airfield and Moody Brook. Airfield desolate, wind swept and enormous breakers on the shore and reef to the east. A large number of Pacara A/Cs there; took photos. Went with Alec Manning [Lieutenant (MCD) and Instructor Officer with the Royal Marines] and helped load MW stores for the MSAs [trawlers]. Had a look round the rusting small arms dump. Saw 4 Exocets on trailers and many AA guns (captured). Moody Brook [Royal Marines barracks at the end of Stanley Water] looked desolate and destroyed by fire. Mud everywhere. Some shopping on the way back. Piggy out with *Diver* [the ex-HMS *Endurance* survey launch we had been given as a diving tender and renamed by the Team]. Lunchtime just stood and observed a gaggle of Cdrs in the bar. Most entertaining. Met a 2-ring RAF Harrier pilot [Flight Lieutenant Mark Hare] with whom I had lunch. Splendid chap. Thinks much as I do. Dhobiing in the

afternoon after 2nd trip to Secretariat. Short snooze. Supper. This evening we had a party in the SAS house ashore. You've never seen so much beer. A good curry too. Music good. Cabaret good. Most of the Team there, who enjoyed it well. No fractions. I left with Dave at around half midnight.

1.7.82 Thursday
Piggy diving on *Tiger Bay* screw change. One man was supposed to supervise the *Atlantic Causeway* suction clearance but nowhere to be found; suspect suffering from last night. I went instead. They were not ready for us which was just as well as it was blowing hard and snowing horizontally. Returned for lunch. Tommo having a 'down' on. We talked about it today and understood one another. We have done some fairly graunchy things together, he and I. *Atlantic Causeway* job finished by dusk having got errant man back. I've said nothing to him, but Piggy has. Taff Reece did the diving. Took the wardroom by surprise this evening with the Cabaret. Played fiddle. Well received. Later had an AAT sesh with QHM and AQHM [AAT: '. . . and another thing! . . .'

2.7.82 Friday
Up early (late) just missed the *Falklands Sound* [captured Argy patrol craft] but she came back to pick me up. Set off for Kidney Island to see the penguins. Negi-birds there so returned. Ian Craig's last trip as Captain. Flew ROMFT [flat hoist which might mean 'Roll on My Fleeting Time', but doesn't] and I played over loudhailer. All the Ships (Merch) gave great reception. Then message to Ship from QHM, 'We've had complaints about your behaviour – cool it!' Which rat pushed his name forward with that one, I wonder. Played him in anyway.
    After lunch Alex and I went walkabout. All Staff-Os

are up meeting Admiral this and that so mess quiet today. Interesting looking at the defences above the town. Wrote to Fiddler and Ma. Video movie, then to bed early.

3.7.82 Saturday

Took Mark Hare, the Harrier Bomber pilot, and 6 of the lads out to see *Hermes* anchored off Seal Island. The sea was quite big out there and there was a snowstorm. She looked very care-worn but still defiant and gave us a wave as we passed. On the way back the port engine of *Diver* overheated and we had to stop it. After lunch and a dhobi, Piggy and I went for a walkabout, saw the Pettersons and watched the parade of Paras, General Moore taking the salute. He looked every inch the fighting General. What a difference to his appearance in the Wardroom, where he looked rather tired. On the way back we found a couple of LCVP Booties working on their engines and invited them to FCDT's Office for a warm and a beer. Quite a little party we had and they're going to fix our port engine for us. Later, after dinner, we all met up again. I've been promising the lads for weeks now, 'Saturday Night in Stanley, down the Pub and I'm playing the Fiddle.' Well, tonight it happened.

It was Saturday night in *RFA Sir Bedivere*, alongside the jetty in Stanley. A group of Very Senior Officers stood by the bar in the mess, and during a lull in the conversation the Commodore asked if I was playing my fiddle ashore that night. 'No, sir. Can't go out after curfew. After eight o'clock you get shot.'

'Curfew?' said an extremely senior Royal Marine officer (Jeremy Moore). 'What's all this about a curfew, Bernie? I never said anything about a curfew!'

'Thank you, sir. I'm on my way.'

We found the Victory Bar open, the only one as it happened, and piled into the fray. The beer did not last long but the rum was plentiful and everyone was in high spirits. There was so little room that I had to stand on a bench to play but that only made the scene better: the fiddler, half seen through a haze of tobacco smoke, above the heads of the packed throng. 'Play us something for the Falklands!' came the demand. Of course one could make up something but never play it the same twice, even if one could remember it. I chose instead to put the 'Nancy's Reel' into march time with a few embellishments and frills of my own. The tune was well accepted amid much stamping of feet and clapping in time.

'What's it called?' came the cry.

'Let's call it "White Flag Over Stanley." ' and so it was.

Some time later the tune was adopted into the repertoire of the Royal Marines Band in Scotland. It was played as I brought HMS *Gavinton* into Rosyth to be finally paid off after 33 years' service.

Back in the Victory it was time to visit the 'head'. Leaving my fiddle in the window, I asked one of the LCVP Royal Marines to guard it until I came back. On returning, I found the young man standing 'properly at ease' in front of the window, growling at the assembled company. 'No one comes near the boss's fiddle', and a small space all around him. I hate to think what would have happened to anyone foolish enough to try their luck. Cheers, Royal!

The first and last opportunity. They have not been open before and we're leaving soon. The only one open was the aptly named 'VICTORY'. Packed, it was, with Paras (noisy), Booties [Royal Marines], sojers, RAF etc. I got to the playing soon enough and got a few tunes in before the Paras started shout/singing. Later however, by dint of standing on a bench, I managed to play the assembled company 'Nancy' (heavily disguised and introduced as 'White Flag Over Stanley'), for the Sgts 'Music while you work' and for the Sprogs 'Pugwash'. All in all very successful. Presented the Landlord with a 'Good ere, Innit!' sticker which he stuck behind the bar with two darts. We all went back to *Sir B* Sgts Mess where Piggy fell over and eventually I left them to it. Good evening. Some snow – Pub ran out of beer – made do with rum.

4rd July
Port Stanley

Dear Ma,

Well, that's it and we are away home. Hopefully we shall fly out in a couple of days. Everything has changed now that peace has broken out and the place is full of staff officers. They look at us rather disapprovingly as we are rather scruffy, having only one set of clothes each and those have been through a bit of a rough time. The semblance of normality that the 'staffies' try to engender, however, cannot dampen the Falklands spirit demonstrated by my boys and our somewhat 'secret' friends. We all feel as though we have been right up close to the edge of life, looked over and then stepped back with a new understanding of reality; something that the 'Johnny Lates' cannot possibly understand.

Winter is well set in now. There is heavy snow that at least keeps the mud at bay and transforms the town into a fresh, clean environment – quite at odds with the scene that greeted us on our arrival. The Argies certainly made a mess of the place. I have met quite a few Islanders, who are very pleasant but rather insular (obviously) in their demeanour. However, we did have one cracking party last night in the first pub to be opened since the surrender. Guess what – the fiddle went down a treat, especially when I conjured up a tune which we called 'White Flag Over Stanley'.

But it is time to come home.

See you soon,
Love,
Nigel

4.7.82 Sunday
Snowing intermittently from showers to blizzard. Everything's gone white. A quiet day spent reading and sleeping. Team cleared screw of the Tug *Lively*. A can with the lads before retiring. Today was officially Sunday Routine. Commander Leese and Lt Cdr Nigel Davies (ex-leader of the Elephant Island Exped) arrived to relieve Chris Meatyard.

5.7.82 Monday
CB changes today. Cracked them all before lunch. Everyone packed and ready to go and willing every Herc down onto the runway.

THE SENIOR LEECH

Should we remark, 'How right you are,'
Or with forthrightness say,
'Despite mistakes we may have made,
It was not done that way;
No doubt you will hypothesize,
Our actions to decry,
But it was we who made the grade -
It was not you, 'twas I.'?

We listen, dutifully bound,
As younger men must do,
While condescending patronage
Our comments honey-dew.
Perhaps he's right, this pedagogue,
Pretentious, unconcerned,
But he had never seen that wreck
From which we had returned.

So, when that breeze of platitudes
Increases to a gale,
When he, unknowing of our part,
Creates some fairy-tale

> Of our attainments, using me
> As springboard to his rank,
> I muse, 'You swill your brandy, pal,
> But it was rum we drank.'

Soon we would be flying out, but each Herky-bird that failed to land because of the snow would put us another day right on the list (i.e. delay us by a further day). The transport aircraft had only a short time to make it, a couple of tries at the most, and then they would have to pull off and back to Ascension Island. Consequently, every time one of these aircraft appeared, all the lads would be out on the jetty with shouts of 'Get it down there!'

'Come on, you can do it.'

'Now, now, put it down.'

'Come on, my son!' All this being accompanied by much waving and flapping of arms.

If ever a group of men could have landed an aeroplane by sheer force of will, my Team were the ones to do it.

Diver topped up with water but got pumped out and the engineers from *Sir B* sorted out the port engine. Lads playing catch with a rugby ball on the jetty. Taff Hurley caught it at his chest, slipped in the snow and fell flat aback. Time to go home, I think.

Up to the 'Victory' again this eve for the Team's last 'run'. Never saw much of the lads as they were down at the other end of the bar. I was playing up by the dart board. There were that many rums coming my way, you would not believe. We followed on to the RCT mess for cabaret etc. but they were all bombed out. In the 'Victory' I met a Fiddler/poet who had come in specially to see me, name of Des Peck. Gave me a copy of his poem 'Surrender of the Argie Forces' and had a bash at the fiddle. Did very well and a good vibrato. More into the old songs though. Nice man. Vivienne, the landlady, looked after us at closing time too. Promised her a tape from the Swan. [On our return to

UK, the band at the Swan recorded a tape for the Victory and included the definitive version of 'White Flag Over Stanley'.] That's important. Ended up in *Sir B's* Sgts Mess for a can.

SURRENDER OF THE ARGY FORCES
(Verses composed by Des Peck, sung to the tune of 'Who wouldn't be lovely')

The Navy are firing all night through,
The planes are bombing the Argies too,
But the Task Force is determined
To see this battle through,
To liberate the Falklands
And restore the Red, White and Blue.

Chorus:
We fought in the mountains
And in the peatbogs too:
The Argies could not stop us
From getting through.
Within two miles of Stanley
The final battle took place;
It looked as if the Argies
Were in a country race.

Verse:
So now the battle is over
And British sovereignty remains;
The Juntas were defeated
Due to lack of brains.
I can see General Galtieri
With fear in his eye,
But like all aggressors
They are doomed to die.

Chorus

6.7.82 Tuesday
Sailed for replenishment in outer harbour at 0800. Piggy plus Team grinding off *Tiger Bay*'s prop [which had a great many 'nicks' in it and required smoothing]. 0930 the IRIS (cable layer) entered, carrying our reliefs. Wrote the Report of Proceedings in forenoon and after a lunch – a video, bath and dhobi. Ship empty of Staff until the evening. Story in latest *Times* saying how Alan Swan, OC RAF Bomb Team, 'slept next to the bombs at Ajax Bay to give the Hospital Staff confidence.' That's news; he was at the other end of the building. It was my lads who slept between the bombs and the hospital.

Piggy not back by 2000 and no sign of our reliefs.

Piggy, Tommo and I went to the SAS house late to help celebrate the promotion to Colonel of the Major. We presented him with three bottles of champagne salvaged from the fire in *Tristram*.

The SAS had decided to have an informal mess dinner to celebrate the promotion to Colonel of their boss. They had not told him about the signal, however, and did not do so until after the meal. We arrived a few minutes beforehand.

When the message had been read and congratulations given, Piggy stepped forward and presented the Colonel with a bottle of champagne from out of the depths of his famous duffle-coat. He was amazed and touched by this gesture from Fleet Team Three, and the more so when Piggy produced a second and then a third.

'But where did you get them?' he asked.

'Aha!' said Piggy, 'these are not ordinary bottles of champagne. We didn't think you would like ordinary bottles of champagne. These bottles of champagne came from the burned-out wine-store in *Tristram* at Bluff Cove. The boys had to put the fire out to get them – and they were still cold!'

The Colonel and everyone were most pleased. It turned out that he was at Wellington and we had a right reunion.

(Wellington College is a public school which specialised, in our day, in producing 'upper-class wide boys'.)

There was some cabaret as usual, and altogether it was a great 'run'. We got a rope round our screw on the way back, but we had a second one, so who cares!

LEAVING

Oh, how I long to see
The colours of England;
Green on green,
Gentled by
The wind-riven rain.
The countryside's alive there,
My spirits will revive there.
Oh, how I long to see
Her rivers once again.

7.7.82 Wednesday
Left the ship at 0745 for shore but it was some time before anyone from FCDT 5 appeared [our relief team of Clearance Divers, upon whom the brunt of the clearing up operation now rested]. Went to the SAS house and had a heart-starter with Fred then met with Alex who took me to greet Steve Field, my relief. Not a lot to hand over, just chat and the drugs [morphine, thankfully not required]. Nigel Davies took the Confidential Books. Rex cleared *Diver*'s screw. We went back to the SAS house where we drank beer and told dits all morning. They cooked us 4 × duck for inflight sarnies [sandwiches]. 1215 mustered on jetty but negi-transport. Broken. SAS put out ambushes and commandeered transport, so eventually arrived at airport.

By midday we were all set to go, gear packed (what there was of it) and Team mustered. Unfortunately the transport to the airfield was broken and we were therefore stuck truckless.

Our friends in the SAS reacted swiftly. Deploying to salient points they invited all transport to take part in a hill climb on the icy road up the slope out of town. The prize: to give FCDT 3 a lift to their flight. Those that succeeded in finishing the course returned to the jetty, picked up the lads and took them away to the airfield. Here many friends came to see us away with an impromptu party.

Then it was time to board the aircraft, and the boys found that their divers' hampers, with their twin wooden bottom-slats, made excellent toboggans on the icy runway. Sadly, they had to be told to cool it, as we were re-entering the world of peace-time service and the Loadmaster would probably throw us off the aircraft if we were seen to be enjoying ourselves. But for a moment, as a last fling, it was fun to watch several Divers hurtling towards the aircraft on their improvised sledges.

Fred plus SAS to see us off, plus MSA [trawler] COs. More beer and eventual in and lift off at 1530. Hurrah!
So that's it. We left Falkland Islands very quietly; just upped and left.

THE MEN OF THE SEA

What men are these who ply the seas,
What forms of self-destruction?
What living symbols of our fate,
What victims of reduction?
What right is given them to kill,
What right for preservation?
What right to take a human life,
What price its conservation?
What knowledge do they use for good,
What knowledge use for evil?
What acts can help? What acts can harm?
What homage pays the Devil?

And when will they be free again,
And will they be contented?
And will they have the life they choose
Or will they be prevented?
And is the rocky land a curse
Or is it just depressing?
And have they left their God behind
Or do they ask his blessing?
So, is the sea their only world
Or is the land their ally?
Or do they wish to turn again
And then repent their folly?

Are they pure kindred to the sea
Or are they souls tormented?
And do they speak their mind out loud,
And is their case presented?
The answers . . . they cannot be told,
The questions . . . answered never.
They are the men who search the seas,
Their quest goes on for ever.

8.7.82 Thursday
I got really hacked off during the flight as, having ensured that everyone else was settled, I found that I had nowhere to sit or lie. Towards midnight this became imperative and I eventually pinched Piggy's pit, he'd been crashed out for 8 hours. So I stretched my back, which was hurting bad, and had an hour. Had a good couple of hours FP earlier. Now at 0230 (Falkland Time) we are approaching Ascension Island.

Straight off the Herc and onto a VC10 with only a short pause to get a 40oz bottle of rum for £3.

Landing at Ascension Island, we were to trans-plane to an RAF VC10 bound for Britain. First, on being diverted to the duty free tent, we were told that we would each be allowed to take two bottles of spirits back to the UK. So, scraping together what money we could, we bought our quota.

As we approached the aeroplane, a chap rushed up and said, 'It's all right, lads, we have informed your next of kin that you are on your way.'

He was mightily surprised when several of the Team turned on him.

'What did you want to do that for?'

'Couldn't you have asked us first?'

'Who said you could, anyway?'

All we wanted to do was to slip quietly into the country with no fuss and no fanfare. Now that was not going to be possible, and we should not be able to pick our own time to face our families again.

We reached the UK and flew into Brize. On the approach the RAF crew told us, 'Now remember, lads, you will be going through customs when you get in. The allowance is one bottle each and no more. If you have any over, you will have to leave it on the plane.'

Here was a turn-up, and us with no cash to pay the extra duty.

We landed and proceeded to 'customs'. This consisted of an officer standing on a chair and saying, 'Has anyone got any firearms or ammunition? No? Right, you are all free to go.'

Unfortunately we were not free to go back to the aircraft to collect our extra booze. I wonder what happened to it.

The Team passed into the arrival area and the cacophony started. There were tears and sobs, red faces and red eyes in the waiting crowd. One of the lads said, 'How come they are not glad to see us? I don't need this!' and tried to get back on the plane. As it turned out, most of the Team was soon scattered to the four winds. I did not get the chance to say farewell, and two of them I was never to see again.

Long flight back to Brize and, on arrival, there were families – tears etc. – and who needed that? Dave Fawsey and Hamish Louden [two Lieutenant-Commanders (MCD) of great experience and expertise] met us. Ma arrived with Brenda Osla but left shortly after as we had no details of what's happening after *Vernon*. But we are back and that's that.

Most of the lads went straight off home from Brize. Never got a chance to thank them. Few of us back to *Vernon* by bus. Arrived in eve. Tom McShee there to greet me and old cabin ready. People in the Bar very kind and talked with young officers on MCD course. Ended up in Night Bar late. So good to be back. Late-on checked lads settled in OK in their mess. Crashed out well.

The arrival back at *Vernon* closed the door on the adventure. The boys that remained went off to their mess and had a party, and I repaired to the wardroom where Mr McShee welcomed me back. The wardroom was quiet, but there were a few people about, notably some young officers on the MCD Long Course. A handful of us ended up in the night bar. Around midnight I sortied to check on the lads and make sure that they were all settled in, and then returned to my old cabin, no 26, which Tom McShee had secured for me. I slept the sleep of the very weary.

Rising early next morning, I luxuriated in a lengthy bath. When I returned to my cabin, it smelled as if something might have died in there. The pong was pronounced, and came from both kit and clothing. I suppose we must have all smelled the same and not realised it. In an environment where dhobi facilities were scarce and kit changes non-existent, it was not surprising that we all took on the odour of half man, half beast. But how kind people are, for no one even hinted at the fact in the bar the night before.

It was very good to be back.

On 9 October 1982, a Friday, the Chief of Staff to Flag Officer Plymouth telephoned to say that I had been awarded the Distinguished Service Cross for my removal of the *Galahad* bomb.

FAME

Solitude's mantle,
Ripped apart by the grasping
Fingers of the mob,
Although retrieved in tatters,
Offers no sanctuary
To shroud our secrets
Nor yet our imperfections.

Envoi: 'WHERE ARE THEY NOW?'

The bottle of 'San Carlos Water' is in the custody of World War Two rear-gunner Harry Hartop, past landlord of the Swan Hotel, and only to be sampled if he, Fiddler and I meet up on 22 June in any year. So far this has only happened once.

The Mad Mean Mine was returned to the UK, where Tommo helped to steam out the explosives. It resides in what used to be HMS *Vernon* and is occasionally wheeled out to be shown to mine warfare trainees.

What is left of HMS *Vernon*, the Torpedo and Anti-Submarine School and the Diving Branch's Alma Mater, is now the satellite of a larger establishment and is called HMS *Nelson* (Gunwharf). Even the name has gone, and it is whispered that the Submariners want it for one of their new 'boats'.

The Falklands fiddle returned to the UK, but lost all its resonance and died. Having been played in the harsh environment of our northern waters, the tropical heat of the Indian Ocean, the baking humidity of the Persian Gulf and the numbing cold of the South Atlantic, it decided that enough was enough and looked for somewhere to rest. Now, complete with its camouflaged case, it can be seen in the Royal Marines Museum at Eastney: a fitting place for it to end its days.

I have since learned that the Defence EOD School has

rigged up a training module in which bomb-disposal students are invited to try their hand at removing highly sensitised 'bombs' from a ship-like environment. The original devices are long gone from *Galahad* and *Lancelot* but the lessons remain to be learned and the skills are yet honed to that perfection that can only have its accolade in the fact that '. . . they didn't go bang.'

I add this final poem from the Falklands, although it was written four years later when I was on my second tour. We recovered the remains of an Argentinian pilot who had crashed into Blue Ridge and lain undiscovered until that time. It was sad that his burial, properly done, was seen by the press as an opportunity to create so much ill will.

BLUE RIDGE PILOT

It is a strange feeling to take a man's hand
In pieces from the peat where it has lain four years,
Scraping his finger bones from the frozen ground
With a bayonet point, to stack them neatly aside.
How odd it is to find his hair still ruffled
In that rocky cranny where the cold wind explores,
And to glean scattered bones, left by scavengers,
Seeking to catalogue his percentage presence.

The wreckage of his plane tells us how he peered
Through the blizzard, to see the ridge looming above;
How he might have cleared the scarp but for the rock,
The outcrop that became his natural tombstone.
But rather than relate the tale, now he makes
His bed in the cold earth of Goose Green cemetery.
Yet there is another, pleasanter feeling,
To know that at last his long vigil is over.

Smith were boat's crew for this phase. On arrival at Fitzroy Sound the mine was anchored well into the sound and left marked and lit overnight.
2. On 26th June a close in-water recce was undertaken by the same team, and detailed measurements and drawings collected. The mine proved to be spherical with the following characteristics:

Top Hemisphere – 5 chemical horns, cover-plate, three lifting/securing eye-plates.
Bottom Hemisphere – 2 chemical horns on welded extensions, with lugs; mechanism plate incorporating mooring-spindle.

No hydrostatic or safe-rendering devices were apparent and the mine was not recognised by any of the team. Later CPO(D) Trotter and LS(D) Thompson from FCDT 3 were flown out with additional equipment and publications. A search through these failed to find any item of similarity between the mine and current information. A further recce was carried out by the FCDT 3 members, with LS(D) Thompson acting as swimmer in this instance. The mine was deemed to be of no known type.
3. During the evening CPO(MW) Marshall and his team constructed a sledge for transportation of the mine from the water on to and over the beach to an area designated for RSP. This piece of equipment consisted of an inverted pallet with a life-ring set into it, resting on and secured to two halves of an oil drum. In the event the *Junella* sledge turned out to be an excellent piece of gear, ideally designed by Marshall for the job.
4. Beaching operations commenced at first light and, with the remote assistance of the ship's MW Ratings, the mine was landed, undamaged, in short order. The depth of water on this shallow beach necessitated the 'walking ashore' of the mine by two swimmers (Bruen and Thompson) to prevent horn damage on the sand-bars,

before an attempt could be made to locate the device upon the sledge. Considerable effort and endurance was required here. The team then returned to HMS *Junella* for RSP planning. Permission having been granted, the FCDT 3 members and CPO(MW) Marshall set off for the beach to complete the task.
5. The RSP was carried out as follows:

   a. Remove base plate and inspect
   b. Remove top plate and inspect
   c. Remove primer cover and inspect
   d. Remove filler cover and inspect
   e. Remove detonator upon identification

   Intelligence suggested that this device might have been fitted with anti-stripping devices or booby traps, and the task was undertaken with this in mind. The RSP took two hours to perform.
6. Eight points secured the base plate, which was located by a lug. One stud was already missing. Five of the nuts were removed by hand and the last two removed explosively. This explosive removal was carried out by CPO(D) Trotter, he having the most experience in the art. The results were excellent, little damage being sustained by the mechanism plate which was removed remotely. Inspection showed that there was an arm that placed either the detonator or the primer into the charge and made the firing circuit. At this stage it was not possible to determine whether the visible charge was detonator or primer, as no leads were seen to connect with it. It was decided to treat it as a primer and to continue the search for the detonator.

   To this end, the top cover-plate was removed, using a hammer and chisel as a starter and finally a remote method of removal. This was carried out after the centre nut of the cover had been remotely removed. Inspection revealed a plate, with central port, in the top of the charge casing. The port was removed to reveal a

APPENDIX 1

The War Reports

The *Galahad* Report

1. A 1,000 lb ex-British bomb, having been dropped at close range, struck *RFA Sir Galahad* under the forward end of the port shade-deck and, after moving forward, lodged in a slightly nose-up attitude, pointing aft, in the battery charging shop. After an initial inspection, the disposal task was started at 2030 on the 25th by a team consisting of:

Lt N A BRUEN RN
L/S (D) THOMPSON
AB (D) WALKER
AB (D) MOTTRAM

2. Initial clearing of debris around the UXB was thoroughly and efficiently carried out by the Team, working in rotation and later in unison, and showed the bomb to be lying wrapped in a double layer of alloy sheet. After consultation with the MEO of *Fearless* and the Chief Engineer of the *RFA*, it was decided not to cut away the decks above, but instead to attempt to effect removal via the hatch to the shade-deck and the companion-way to the vehicle-deck. Beam clamps and chain tackles having been provided, the two support teams retired, as advised, to the safety of a lifeboat tethered astern, while the Team started the move.
3. The bomb was slung using a wire strop aft and a helo

strop forward. This last was located and backed-up by man-made-fibre rope-lashings, as the curvature of the nose and the angle of the weapon suggested that some slipping might occur. This work, and indeed the clearance of the debris, was made more difficult by the presence of broken batteries and carboys, and of acid that had been liberally distributed around the compartment on bomb-impact.

4. The UXB was lifted, along with its alloy wrapping, taking care to keep it at the same angle to the horizontal. It was not possible to do any of the move remotely, owing to the necessity to steady the bomb and guard against any undue vibration, as the weight came off some metal sheets, under and around the weapon, that were under stress. The bomb once lifted, the metal wrapping was gently slid off. This took about 20 minutes to achieve. The bomb was then transferred under the hatch and lashed, as the rising wind and sea state were imparting movement to the weapon.

5. A volunteer RCT crane driver now closed up and was directed to hoist the weapon through the two hatches, across the upper deck and to lower it into the waiting Gemini. This operation took some time owing to the weather factor and a malfunctioning crane. The Gemini, filled with cornflakes packets and life-jackets to absorb any shock from the now improving weather conditions, was towed by Thompson and Mottram to deep water where the bomb was allowed to slide over the side of the Gemini. This improvised action concluded the task at 0315 on the 26th May 1982.

6. Leading Seaman Thompson is to be commended for his coolness and efficiency as well as his leadership during the whole operation.
   Able Seamen Walker and Mottram conducted themselves with enthusiasm and cheerfulness in the highest traditions of the Service.

7. Valuable back-up support was provided by the *RFA* Engineering Staff and the Engineering Team from HMS

Fearless. The RCT Crane Driver (unfortunately name unknown) is to be commended for his professional skill and level-headedness during the difficult lift phase.

28th May 1982
RFA Sir Lancelot

The *Lancelot* Report

1. After an initial pre-clearance and inspection, EOD clearance work commenced at 1200 on 28th May. The team consisted of:

   Lt N A BRUEN RN
   CPO (D) G M TROTTER
   LS (D) P M KEARNS
   LS (D) C A SMITHARD
   AB (D) G R WEIR
   AB (D) M A WHEELER
   AB (D) D WALTON

2. The large number of personnel required was due to the complexity of the rigging. CPO Trotter led the operation, calling on Lt Bruen for assistance in close-in work and rigging.
3. The bomb was located in the film store amongst a great deal of debris, which had to be cleared before shoring could be undertaken, and surrounding bulkheads were in an unreliable state. It was decided to remove the welded metal stair under which the bomb was resting, the entire Third Officer's cabin and the outside bulkhead, to provide a removal route. This task was carried out by two Shipwrights from *Intrepid* and *Fearless*, MEA2 D G Farquar and MEMN1 A G Siddle, who should be commended for the outstanding performance of their duties in close proximity to the UXB.

4. Removal of the weapon was complicated by the lack of strong points in the superstructure, lack of cranage and, in the final stage, fierce squalls which hindered the sheer-leg operations. Notwithstanding these problems, the clearance was completed by 1000 on 29th May, when the bomb was lowered to the sea bed, having been hoisted on deck from the centre of the ship, transferred by a series of davits to the upper deck, and lowered five decks to the water-line and beyond.
5. Slinging arrangements for the bomb were similar to those used in the *Sir Galahad* clearance, the bomb itself being of the same type and specification.
6. The support members of the team worked extremely well, as can be seen from the short time taken for such a complex operation.

CPO (D) G M TROTTER
Red Beach One
2 June 82

Note by OiC FCDT 3

CPO Trotter's drive and resourcefulness during this operation were a credit to his rate and branch.

The *Mine* Report

1. On 25th June 1982 HMS *Pict* swept a buoyant chemical-horn mine off the east coast of the Falklands. HMS *Junella* was detailed to take the device in tow to Fitzroy Sound and then anchor it in preparation for investigation and later RSP. The mine was attached by bridle to a towing hawser by a swimmer in high, breaking seas and strong winds. These conditions occasioned both mine and swimmer to be tumbled considerably, but the tow was passed and eventually taken by the ship. CPO(MW) Marshall and LS(MW)

primer block within. The plate was freed of securing nuts but refused to move. The nuts were replaced.

It was now decided to remove the wing-nut that held the movable primer in place. This was done and revealed what could have been the detonator. However, a complete inspection was not possible owing to the limited movement of the charge. The bottom plate of the main charge case was now removed revealing cast explosive. The cover was replaced. Attention was now directed back to the detonator/primer and it was found, after some experimentation, that the carrying tube could be moved into the main charge, thus allowing enough space to extract the small charge. On removal this was identified as the detonator.

7. The mine was now reassembled and moved on the sledge, by the four members of the team, to the water where the sledge was removed and the mine towed at length back to the support ship. Here it was hoisted and re-secured to the sledge on the sweep-deck. The Hertz horns were later removed for safe stowage and a safety certificate given to the Captain.

8. Inspection revealed that, when swept, providing corrosion and sea-growth does not prevent the mooring spindle from retracting, the mine is safe, owing to the detonator being removed and the circuit broken. RSP should consist of removing the base plate, removing the wing-nut, sliding the detonator tube inwards and removing the detonator. If the marine growth prevents the spindle from retracting, the horns should be removed first, providing they are in good condition. This should only be attempted in extremity, however.

9. CPO(D) Trotter's expertise and advice proved extremely useful in this instance, particularly his handling of the explosive removal of the two studs and nuts with minimum damage to the mechanism plate. He has once again been of great credit to the Branch

CPO(MW) Marshall provided invaluable service as recorder and interpreter of the mine workings. He is to be commended for his enthusiasm and hard work in every phase of the operation.

LS(D) Thompson provided valuable support and encouragement. He carried out all the duties assigned to him with the utmost vigour and determination.

28th June 1982
Port Stanley

POSTSCRIPT

The business of 'hands-on' mine disposal is a rare and exacting occupation: the apogee of the bomb-disposal game. Its successful outcome invariably used to result in the highest award available to the civilian honours system. Some time after my encounter with the Argentinian mine, I learned that I had indeed been 'written up' for such an award, but on the military side. As the event took place after hostilities were terminated, I was given to understand that the citation was therefore invalid and, in consequence, discarded. However, it is nice to know that our efforts were in some measure appreciated.

There were many servicemen in the Falklands conflict whose gallant and, indeed, valorous actions merited such distinction. That these remained unreported and therefore unrecognised, is merely part of the fortunes of war. It is enough that they gave of their best and that the outcome was victory.

For they were the sons of warriors who took up the mantle of their sires and, never doubting, strode away to serve their country when she called.

No man can offer more.

APPENDIX 2

The People

> 'I looks towards you all,' says I,
> 'And raise my glass and drink it dry.'
> (B. Bruen)

Fiddler
Jim Jennings, better known simply as Fiddler, was invalided out of the Royal Marines as a Colour-Sergeant after an accident during a helo assault. He was told that he would never walk again but, through courage and great tenacity, he proved this prediction incorrect. He is well remembered in the Corps as the skipper of the Royal Marines Yacht *Sea Soldier*, and by all as a virtuoso fiddle-player – hence his sobriquet. For many years he has been my close friend and 'sea father' and his example, kindness and leadership have been an inspiration to many.

Martin Holloway
An MCD Lieutenant-Commander, Martin Holloway was the 'boss' of the Squadron of Minesweeping Trawlers. Under his leadership they not only cleared the minefields off Stanley but, during the conflict, carried out many hazardous operations, the details of which may never be known. Hopefully these few words will in some part provide the recognition he so well deserves but which has so far eluded him.

Chris Meatyard
As MCD Staff officer to Commodore Amphibious Warfare,

Chris Meatyard was our 'tasker'. He spent much of his time changing between *Fearless* and *Intrepid* to ensure that he was always in the right place and close to his two Fleet Clearance Diving Teams. Always cheerful and helpful (and in possession of an enviably superb black foul-weather overall) he was always there with the goods and a great support to Team Leaders.

Mick Fellows
A senior Warrant Officer Diver, second in command of FCDT 1 and already holder of the British Empire Medal for gallantry, Mick Fellows was the first Warrant Officer to be awarded the Distinguished Service Cross. Heavily involved in bomb disposal and removal, and other diving activities, he was the mainstay of the CD effort in the war. Later he was made MBE for running the Royal Navy's part in the Zeebrugge ferry disaster operation, and he consequently became the most highly decorated Warrant Officer in the armed services.

Piggy
Graham Trotter, known as Piggy, Chief Petty Officer Diver, second in command of FCDT 3 and of vast experience, was the linchpin upon which the Team functioned. Always wearing his famous World War 2 naval duffle-coat, he was involved in every Team event and ensured that everything ran exactly right. Awarded the Distinguished Service Medal for his removal of the 1,000 lb bomb from *RFA Sir Lancelot*, he also master-minded all the diving on the wreck of *Antelope* and gave invaluable assistance in rendering safe the mine. A good friend and companion, he is the epitome of the finest Chief CD 1.

Tommo
Somehow it seemed that wherever I went the black-bearded figure of Tommo was always along too. We had a rapport between us that is seldom found between two men and was

perhaps the result of sharing the same dangerous game – a kind of telepathy. I could not have wished for a finer companion in this adventure. Tommo's Mention in Dispatches was richly deserved for he did more than enough to earn it. On the night in 1983 when I presented the Swan Hotel with a copy of John Lawyer's inspired picture 'All Clear', as I was making the presentation Tommo walked in out of the blue. There was no way he could have known about it, yet there he was and a memorable party ensued. Although a couple of inches under six feet, Tommo is stocky and immensely strong. Such is his personality and presence that the next day the talk of the pub was of the 'huge fellow' from the night before.

Tex Marshall
'Tough as Teak' Tex Marshall (a triple F: Falklands Freedom Fighter) was an old friend from boxing days; he represented his service in that sport for nine years and was known as 'the iron man of the navy squad'. One of the most experienced of the Mine Warfare Chiefs, he was a superb seaman and rigger and a great asset to us when dealing with the sea mine.

Phil
Phil, who was Mentioned in Dispatches for his part in the *Lancelot* clearance, made sure from the start that we were all as fit as possible and in the best condition to meet the rigours that we were likely to face in the war zone. He spent a great deal of time diving on the wreck of HMS *Antelope* and recovering gear from her. As one of the four 'leaders' (leading seamen) on the Team, he was very much at home swept up in the events of the moment.

Chas
Also Mentioned in Dispatches, and one of the same bomb-clearance team, was Chas. He was a little older than the others and had a steadying influence on the younger men.

He was an excellent diver and seaman, and it was with a deep sense of loss that the Diving Branch learned of his death shortly after these events. Chas will long be remembered by all who knew him, and a memorial has been raised to him at Horsea Island, the 'home' of all Divers.

Charlie
The Buffer and procurer for the unit was the 'leader' Charlie. He was a cheerful soul, full of fun and with the knack, possessed only of a few, of ensuring that the Team had as much gear as he could muster. Ask Charlie for a camp-stove or a sleeping mat, and within a short period there it was, more usually than not with a "Sign here, please." Also an accomplished diver, he spent much time surveying the *Antelope* and clearing ordnance around Red Beach.

Jock R
Jock R, always good-humoured, kept up our spirits and was involved in all major diving tasks. He was particularly useful in the hospital, facing unpleasant duties with stoicism and helping out where he could. He came with us to *Sir Tristram* at Bluff Cove, proving there what an accomplished fire-fighter he was to boot.

Jock W
Jock W, a stalwart member of the Team, helped take the bomb out of Lancelot, and of course was involved in much diving work. It was he who led the take-over of the treatment of Bluff Cove burn victims, bringing them relief and showing great compassion and fortitude while doing so; thus were he and his mates able to relieve a number of the medics who were urgently needed elsewhere.

Taff Rees
Very quiet but an absolute powerhouse, despite his small

stature, Taff Rees was a tireless worker who was always there when needed. He undertook any job going, no matter what: from hazardous diving to latrine digging, Taff was the man on the spot, quietly beavering away. That he should be killed by a hit-and-run driver shortly after returning to the UK was a tragic injustice.

Whiskey
Whiskey was a marvel. A strong, fit young man, very level-headed and a first-class diver, he was one of the first into the bomb removal business in *Galahad* and again down at Bluff Cove in *Tristram*. When not involved in other tasks, he made it his job to do as much as possible to improve the facilities at the BMA, and many will remember his constant 'part-time' work there as well as his meticulous care of casualties. He was of the best stamp of clearance diver, and I was glad to have him at my side in a dangerous situation.

Buster
Buster was also there in *Galahad* and completed that team. He and Whiskey were close friends, that friendship having been forged around their 'Big Bad Bomb'. Another who was very much involved in the care of the injured, he was always good-humoured and resourceful, and a pleasure to work with. It was very gratifying to be able to report to the Admiralty that both his and Whiskey's actions were 'in the highest tradition of the service'.

Wheels
Wheels distinguished himself in many ways. From diving tasks to nursing, he was always at the forefront. He was part of the *Lancelot* team, and in the hospital his personal contribution on the night of the Bluff Cove attack will long be remembered. That night he was present in the operating theatre, actively helping the surgeons at the tables. Where every man was needed, it was his forethought in preparing himself for such an eventuality that really paid off.

John Boy
Our mascot was John Boy. Never without a smile, or those trainers of his, he buoyed up morale no end. Even at his lowest ebb, when he was struck down, he still cracked a joke and raised a laugh. A hard-working diver and part of the *Lancelot* team, John Boy was Mentioned in Dispatches for his contribution to the Team's successes.

Joe
On one occasion mistaken for an escaped prisoner, Joe was young-looking and small, but as tough as they come. Air raids, bombings, short rations or miserable conditions did nothing to dampen his spirits. He was an excellent example to his team-mates and a tireless worker. He made himself very useful when the casualties came in, with the building of the blast-wall and during diving operations.

Rex
Rex was another of the younger men who gave everything he could to the job in hand. Although quiet to start with, by the end of it all he had grown in stature and experience. His contribution was on a par with the others but, like Taff Rees, in an unassuming way he provided that back-up so necessary in a Team like ours.

Taff Hurley
Taff Hurley loved it all. He was in his element, and I only heard him complain when he reckoned that he was not getting enough action. He photographed everything avidly and was fascinated by the whole concept of war. It was he who was largely responsible for the Team's preparedness for some of the unpleasant things it came across, particularly the injuries of the wounded, and for its forward thinking. He was also my unofficial 'conscience'. and pleased I was to have him in the Team.

Dave
Then there was Dave. A technical Chief Petty Officer, he

looked after our engines and gear and was guardian of Fort Thompson. Always there with comforts for the lads, the right piece of kit or a quick repair job, he was our 'father confessor' and the sheet-anchor of the Team.

They were a grand bunch of men to take to war and I could not have wished for better. It was gratifying to hear later that, in addition to the awards and 'mentions in dispatches' already noted, six members of the Team received commendations from Commander-in-Chief Fleet for the excellence of their conduct under dangerous conditions.

APPROACH TO THE GREEN

I look across the chart that is my life
And see, like ports and harbours, little creeks and streams,
All the happy times and oft the ones of strife
That filled me with a joy of living and of dreams.
Yet, many lying soft like pools of misty grey,
But half remembered, never whole and clear to see,
Quietly and unnoticed, slide away
And softly lock their doors and hide away the key.

No more shall they be seen, nor bide
With me, that others share what I still know they are.
Like unknown shadow shapes of eventide
They fly, they fade in misty dreams afar.
And as I drift and let life slide me by,
So one by one each hatch is shut and locked and barred;
'Til only one direction, one last door I spy
And there a shining figure, sword in hand, stands guard.

APPENDIX 3

The Cabaret

Songs and stories that were popular 'down south'.

HORSEA ISLAND SONG
(to the tune of Flanders and Swan's 'The Hippopotamus Song')

    All diving officers invariably find
    That a mud run is good for the soul;
    CD Petty Officers instil in their mind
    It will help reach their ultimate goal.
    They sweat and they swear and their temperatures rise
    As they struggle through treacle-like slime;
    For weak and for strong, they all know this song,
    And sing it 'most all of the time.

    Mud, mud, black Horsea mud,
    Nothing quite like it for heating the blood;
    So come from the dry land down to the Island,
    And there let us try our 'and at Horseaous mud.

    Soft black and sticky, it comes up to your knees
    And occasionally up to your waist.
    If you taste an icky-bit, don't swallow it, please,
    For it has a peculiar taste.
    Don't stop or you'll sink, don't sit or slow down,
    Keep moving, whatever the pain;

Or else, have no doubt, you'll soon hear the shout
Of the Chief calling, 'Go round again!'

Mud, mud, black Horsea mud.
Nothing quite like it for heating the blood;
So come from the dry land, down to the Island
And there let us try our 'and at Horseaous mud.

BB

BERNIE'S STORY

(Given to me by Fiddler just before leaving, this story relies heavily on actions and, updated, was immensely popular during the conflict.)

Down at Goose Green, an Argentinian officer is putting out sentries around the perimeter. He places his last man by a river and instructs him that he is not to leave his post until relieved.

All morning the sentry marches up and down on his side of the water, watching for the enemy. Nothing and no one approaches.

Lunch-time arrives and still he paces his beat, peering about, searching the other side. Still nothing.

A little after two o'clock a Royal Marine comes yomping over the hill beyond the stream and spots the Argy.

'Aha!' he says to himself, 'An Argy!' (because he is an intelligent-type Royal Marine). Moving a little closer, he examines the specimen in more detail but does not recognise the uniform. The sentry ignores the Bootie.

'I wonder what kind of Argy it is,' muses the Royal. 'Best ask it; but I don't speak Argy. Sign language – that's the answer.'

So, approaching the water-way, he shouts across to the sentry, 'Oi! Argy! What unit do you belong to, eh? You, what unit you from?'

No reply; so, stretching out both arms horizontally to the

side and tucking his head into his shoulders, the Royal Marine makes like an aeroplane and shouts, 'Are you in the Air Force? You – in – Air Force?'

The sentry affects not to notice the Bootie and continues his pacing.

'H'm!' thinks the Royal. 'He's obviously not in the Air Force; perhaps he's in the Navy.'

Now, making Australian-crawl-like motions with his arms, he shouts out, 'You – in – Navy? Naveee? You – in – Navy?'

Nothing – no response at all.

'Perhaps he's a Marine,' muses the Royal; so, making an aggressively sexual motion upward from the waist with his forearm and clenched fist, he calls across, 'Are you a Marine, then? Eh? Marine?'

With no reaction at all, the sentry continues his patrol, watching our friend from the corner of his eye.

'Well, there's only one unit left,' determines the Jolly, and, miming the action of adjusting a binocular focus and then pulling the instrument away and down from his face, he demands, 'Are you in the Observer Corps?'

The sentry sees this, jumps back, drops his musket and disappears at a rate of knots over the hill towards his base. After a little he is brought to a halt by his officer who grabs him by the throat and growls, 'I told you to patrol that bank until you were relieved. What are you doing here, and where's your musket?'

The sentry gabbles at him in Argy; here is the translation:

'This Royal Marine comes over the hill, down to the bank. He looks across at me and says (he mimics the Bootie's sign language), "At quarter to three," (arms outstretched) "I'm gonna swim across this river," (Australian crawl), "and then I'm gonna * * * * you," (rude gesture with forearm), "until your bloody eyes drop out!" (binocular action) – And there's only five minutes to go!'

DIVER, DIVER!

Chorus:
Diver, diver, show us yer leg,
Show us yer leg, show us yer leg;
Diver, diver, show us yer leg,
A yard beneath the sea.

The CD gets a lot of pay,
Ship's Divers don't get much.
The others have to pay their way,
Like Scooby-doos and such.

The CD swims in a rubber bag,
The SDs too, you bet.
The others swim in nothing at all,
They just get soddin' wet (and cold).

The CD uses pure O_2
And mixy-gas or air.
The others, they use CO_2;
We got no air to spare.

The CD drinks his ale and beer,
Scrumpy, rum and grog.
The others drink peculiar things
Like cocktails and eggnog.

BB

PIGGY'S STORIES

There was once a mathematician who wanted to build a low wall around his patio. Being a man of intelligence, with a precise nature, he worked out beforehand just how much sand and cement he would need and the exact number of bricks required. Legging it round to the local

DIY centre, he asked for 143 bricks.

'We only sell them by the dozen,' said the salesman. 'You'll have to have 144.'

'But I only need 143,' rejoined the mathematician, 'I have worked it all out very carefully and I only need 143.'

'I am sorry,' repeated the salesman, 'we only sell them by the dozen, so you will have to take a gross.'

By now the man was getting angry. 'Look! I want 143 bricks, not 144. I do not want the extra brick. I have no use for it.'

'I am very sorry, sir, but we only sell by the dozen, so you will have to take it.'

'But what am I supposed to do with the extra brick?'

'That is not my concern, sir; you can do with it as you will.'

'Right!' said the customer, and tearing the offending brick from the package, he hurled it with all his might straight up into the air.

★ ★ ★

No? Well, we never understood it either. We heard it several times, but somehow the point of it evaded us. Piggy's other story was, however, a little different – though not much.

★ ★ ★

A salesman went on his holidays and, not having a great deal of time off, decided to go by air. On the other side of the aisle there was a little old lady with a fluffy, white miniature poodle, sitting next to a very large, overweight American. Hardly had the flight started than the American pulled out an oversize cigar and proceeded to light it, amid much coughing, spluttering and smoke. This upset the old lady and started the dog yapping. A violent altercation then occurred between the old lady, the American and the dog.

'Will you stop that blasted dog from yapping.'

'Put out your cigar. That's what's doing it, so put it out.'

'No, you stop that blistering row.' And so forth.

The upshot of it all was that the little old lady grabbed the man's cigar and threw it out of the window. The American reacted immediately by throwing the poodle out of the window. The old lady had hysterics and fainted, and the plane suddenly juddered and screamed down to make an emergency landing.

As he was leaving the aircraft, the salesman looked back – and what do you think he saw sitting on the tailplane?

(Answers would now come thick and fast.)

'The dog?'
'No.'
'The cigar?'
'No.'
'The dog and the cigar?'
'No.'
'The dog *smoking* the cigar?'
'No.'
'Well, what then?'
'The brick; the one he had sold the mathematician!'

CLEARANCE DIVERS' SONG
(to the tune of 'The Ash Grove')

When we started diving
We were told that conniving
Was certainly thriving
Among the CDs.
A brass one and a copper one,
A small one and a whopper one,
A momma one and a poppa one
They filched from the seas.
And the air from his suit-inflation;
And the air from his suit-inflation,
And the air from his suit-inflation
Went up to his knees.
A copper one and a brass one,
And a sticky-icky on the last one,
And the air from his suit-inflation
Went up to his knees.

BB

FRED'S STORY

'I dreamed of you last night, Fred.'
'Really? What happened?'
'Well, I was in the Devil's waiting room and the Devil came in, swinging his tail. He climbed up on to a platform and started to read names out of a big book. As each name was read out, a figure would detach itself from the milling throng and go through one of the great bronze doors that surrounded the place. We would get glimpses of chains and red-hot irons, whips and fire, and could hear the cries of the tormented. This was very obviously Hell.

'Then he read out my name. I went forward and said to him,

"I think there must have been a mistake. I'm not supposed to be down here. I've always been a decent, clean-living lad. I should be in the other place, not down here."

"There's no mistake,' answered the Devil, glaring down, 'Your name's in the book and in you go."

"Well, I ain't going, and that's that."

"But you've got to go. Your name's in the book."

"No, there is no way I'm going through those doors."

"You really mean it, don't you?" The Devil looked amazed.

"Well, if you really are that serious . . . ."

"I am."

"There is one way. Do you see that, over there?"

I looked and saw a hideous female goblin slavering in the corner.

"If you can become intimate with that, then you may go free."

Horrible though the thought was, I knew that I must succeed; so, putting a paper bag over my own head, I turned-to.

After a time, I was aware of moanings coming from round the corner. These were so persistent that I left off my own activities in order to take a peek.

There was you, Fred, and Bo Derek! I rushed up to the Devil and demanded, "What the .... is going on? How come I get the goblin and Fred gets Bo Derek?"

"Ah well," replied the Devil, "You see, Bo Derek wants to get out of here as well."

DIVER'S SONG
(to the tune of 'A Policeman's lot is not a Happy One')

I'm a diver, I'm for diving and my buddy
Gives me the helping hand that I require;
For when I'm down the bottom where it's muddy,
He'll haul me up in case I should expire.
And later we'll go down unto the alehouse
To find out how much beer we can consume.
Yes, together we'll go to the beer-retail-house
And we'll stay there all the bloody afternoon.

Chorus:
Yes, we'll all go down unto the nearby alehouse
And we'll stay there all the bloody afternoon.

Now the boss has got himself a little notebook
And in it he writes down the time we spends
With our breathing-sets beneath the rippling waters,
And who is who and who that who attends.
He writes down all the info on the pages
And we don't worry, cos we know that soon
He will look and see we've been down there for ages
And he'll haul us up before the afternoon.

Chorus:
Yes, we'll all go down unto the nearby alehouse
And we'll stay there all the bloody afternoon.

Sometimes you'll find a girl-friend, wife or mother
Will come out in our boat to see us dive;
And she'll marvel at our care for one another
As we make sure that we all remain alive;
But she may think there's trouble or there's danger,
As for astronauts who walk upon the moon,
So we'll take her down the pub and there we'll range her,
Cos we'll stay there all the bloody afternoon.

Chorus:
Yes, we'll all go down unto the nearby alehouse
And we'll stay there all the bloody afternoon.

BB

APPENDIX 4

A Career Remembered

The letter, written to the Tutor of Orange Dormitory at Wellington College, which started me on the compilation of this book.

Sultanate of Oman
11 February 1989

Dear Mr Baker,
It occurred to me, after receiving your letter, for which I thank you, that students probably fail to keep their tutors appraised of their doings, in much the same way as sailors drop from our ken once they leave our ships. I have perhaps been luckier than most, in that many of my men have kept in touch and I have been able to watch them grow in position and stature, albeit from a distance. Therefore, if you will forgive my ramblings, I shall over the next few days pound out (two-fingered) on my cheap Chinese portable some thoughts of yesteryear.

On leaving Wellington I did not immediately join the Royal Navy, as that door had been closed to me by the Master at my first attempt. I think that he wrote, 'I would not trust this boy with a bicycle, let alone a helicopter.' He was probably right. Thus, after 'O' levels, I went out into the world to seek my fortune.

Initially, as a change from ten years of boarding school, I stayed at home and tried various jobs, ranging from selling encyclopaedias to running a tie factory – or at least helping to run one. I was also employed as a waiter, a painter, a music shop assistant, a farm labourer and a repossessor of television sets. After an unfortunate incident in Trafalgar Square when John Bowley, Tony Trembeth, Mike Henderson, Jim Darley and I were unaccountably attacked by a large number of youths, I ended up in hospital in a critical state. Upon recovery I quit the country and went to live in a non-English-speaking district of France, where my farming experience came much to my aid.

After a few months I returned to the UK, having forgotten much of my English, and enrolled in the Birmingham School of Drama, under the direction of the redoubtable Miss Pam Chapman. I stayed for a year and qualified as an assistant stage manager. Once again I set off into the world to try my destiny. I worked in the Manchester Library Theatre, the Belgrade Theatre in Coventry, and in a most peculiar tour of Northern Ireland with Pinter's *The Caretaker* performed by the Welsh Theatre Company. Then I 'rested'. It came to us all eventually. However, I happened to get in touch with David Gordon, the stage director and producer at the Midlands Art Centre under Sir John English. I had been lent to him earlier by the School to help run the opening by Princess Margaret, and I had conceived and worked the lighting plot. It was one of those fortuitous and fortunate telephone conversations that started with, 'Hello David, you are not looking for a good stage manager by any chance, are you?' He replied that he was, and I was given a month's trial. Unfortunately there was no pay until the end of the month, and by that time I was reduced to living on dried meat and water. My month of trial over, I was accepted, and there started a splendid period of my life that I still look back upon with fondness and pride.

I had managed to jump about five years of the normal ASM career path, and was given the immensely challenging job of running the theatre, teaching lighting, acting and stage management, and assisting in the teaching of mime under that wonderful artist Geoff Buckley.

The theatre was a studio version and had all the absolutely latest equipment, particularly in the lighting field. The world was our oyster and experimentation was the name of the game. I was required to work with many people, some famous at the time, others to achieve their accolades later, but the people that I most enjoyed working with were the young of Birmingham, although I was scarcely older. One in particular, who showed great talent and with whom I have remained in friendship, was Simon Barron, now one of the 'names' in Hollywood, where he is a director.

With all the enthusiasm of the young and the unlimited use of equipment, it is hardly surprising that I formed a love affair with the technique of lighting. Great things were happening in this field in the sixties, and we were right up there at the top. Eventually I decided to go my own way and start up a special effects lighting firm – LX84 by name. But before I left the Arts Centre, I was allowed to produce and direct my own show, an experimental work of originality and great beauty. I can safely say that no one in the country had reached the standard that we attained that night, and the critics were favourably impressed. Most importantly however, my father, though very ill at the time, was able to attend, and saw that perhaps his son had not wasted his life after all. Shortly afterwards he died. This, of course, was a great blow to us all, and even today my mother has never regained that gay demeanour that made her so well loved.

Now I left behind me the security of a paid job, the joy of working with such people as John Blundell the puppet-master, and the ordered life of the theatre. This time I was truly on my own and should stand or fall by my endeavours. – I fell.

Artistically what we produced was the best in the country, but one has to market something as new as this was, and that I had not the experience to do, nor the financial independence to achieve. The assignments we managed to find were largely in the pop music world. We were able to work in a very exciting environment with interesting people, and work we did – hard.

Eventually we got our big break and were engaged to provide the Hytesenemic (visual sound) lighting for a ten-hour gala pop concert in Birmingham's Bingley Hall, featuring the very top groups of the day. We filled that hall with a 360° coverage of moving light: an estimated 650,000 sq ft. It was a great success and acclaimed by the press as a significant advance, even on the Roundhouse, famous as the leading exposition of 'light' in London. Unfortunately the organisers of the event took off and were never heard of again, and I was well out of pocket. In order to pay off my operators and costs, I had to sell my equipment and car. Looking back, I can see now that there were other ways, but at the time that was how it worked out.

When one door closes another usually opens, and I applied to join the Royal Navy as a Short Service helicopter pilot. I passed the flying aptitude tests, largely on my father's reputation I believe, and went on to the Admiralty Interview Board. This I passed also. They perhaps thought that I was a little unusual for, instead of giving the normal type of answer to the question, 'What is your ambition in the Royal Navy?', I answered that I wished to become 'a recognised expert in my own field.' It was during this episode that one of my fellow candidates, Corporal Paul Jenner RM, gave me the nickname 'Bernie': as he put it, 'I am a Royal Marine. I cannot call you Nigel.' Since then I have always been known by my nickname in naval circles, and by my given name in others.

Dartmouth was wonderful. Above all I enjoyed the practical aspects of the training: the boatwork, seamanship, fire-fighting, practical leadership and the like. The academic work I found hard. I was most surprised to receive two gifts of money from Wellington to help me through my training. One was for being the best OW [Old Wellingtonian] cadet at BRNC that year, and the other informed me that, as my father had recently died, I was technically a Foundationer and entitled to help for the period of my stay. This was a very kind thought, and also most welcome.

I started my flying training, but soon found that flying was not for me. I did not like it at all. Consequently I transferred to the Seaman Branch and took an interest in diving; quite by accident as it happens. My Divisional Officer told me that I spent altogether too much time on the river (!) and that I was to find myself another interest. I happened upon diving, and before long was qualified as a Ship's Diving Officer while still a cadet – my first taste of HMS *Vernon*, the establishment that was to figure so largely in my life.

We spent one term in the Dartmouth Training Squadron working as both sailors and officer cadets. I was in HMS *Tenby* and enjoyed our hard-working cruise around the Mediterranean immensely, despite falling foul of our part-of-ship Leading Hand at an early stage. This was Leading Seaman Topsy Turner who, after giving me a hard time for three months, declared that I had done well and gave me his 'tot of rum'; about as good an accolade as a sailor could give. Perhaps he was impressed by the care I lavished on the ship's Montague whaler, for which I had a great regard and fondness.

I applied to transfer to the Royal Marines, that I might join the SBS. After all, here I was a ship's diver, mountaineer, canoe instructor (I had qualified while instructor at TS VAGA in Hereford a year or so before), thoroughly at home with boats and all things practical, and a marksman to boot. It seemed the logical step. The Training Officer agreed, as did the First Lieutenant. The Captain did not, and explained to me that, in order to proceed, I would first have to resign from the RN (no return) and then apply as a civilian, as there was no way that I could transfer directly. Secondly, he told me, I was too old and so would not get in anyway. It was not until I returned to Dartmouth and discussed the matter with the Captain RM that I discovered that I had been misinformed, and could in fact have transferred direct.

What is more, he would have made strong recommendations for such a transfer. By this time, however, it was too late.

I passed out of Dartmouth, and the great door slammed with a reverberating boom behind us. True to tradition, we all let forth a cheer and hurled our new caps in the air. A new life.

My first proper ship was HMS *Brinton*, under the command of a Fleet Air Arm Gannet pilot, the last left alive of his batch. He was one of the nicest of men, Lieutenant-Commander Paul Bootherstone, later to be awarded the DSO in the Falklands conflict. *Brinton* was a member of the 9th Mine Countermeasures Squadron, based in Bahrain. She was a Ton Class minesweeper, recently converted to mine-hunter, and the Squadron was under the command of the remarkable Commander John Gunning. I spent six months in the ship as the Midshipman, one of five officers. I was the Gunnery Officer and had a Bofors gun of 40mm calibre as my main armament, a 20mm Oerlikon as secondary, and a rack of small arms for close-in work.

We 'hunted' the Gulf shipping routes and patrolled off Muscat and Oman, where the young Sultan Qaboos was fighting a war to oust the Yemenis from his country. Those hours spent 'hunting' were to bear fruit in the late eighties, when information we had gathered was to form the basis for the mine clearance of tanker routes and anchorages during the closing stages of the Iran-Iraq war. During my time on board, the ship visited Kuwait, Bombay, Cochin, Colombo, Penang and Singapore, where she was refitted. I left her there and returned to the UK, to join another ship for the second half of my Mid's time and Promotion Board.

'M1114 HMS *Brinton*' (an excerpt)

I stand. I stare. I look. I see
A beauty made for men with minds of steel,
A sound to reach the pitying ear

And maybe set the soul afire;
A colour, all as one and never dead,
A colour live to all experience.

I stand. I hear. I smell. I feel
A world of violence, yet unborn;
A small and frail, forgotten craft,
Waiting like her sisters,
Ships of Ostend and Zeebrugge.

HMS *Albion* was an aircraft carrier converted to carry a full Commando of Royal Marines anywhere in the world and there to support them in a limited war role. I joined her at Invergordon and we set off to the Mediterranean for exercises. She was commanded by Captain Henry Leech, who later became First Sea Lord.

The Midshipmen, of whom there were about 14, lived in one of the last gunrooms in the Navy, and we had a high old time. The accent was on studying for the Fleet Board and learning all those things that had been impossible while working hard in an MCMV. We kept bridge watches, boiler-room watches, gangway watches and deck watches. We became conversant with stores, guns, aircraft, navigation, signals, double bottoms, damage control, anchors and cables, and – above all – boats. We landed with the Royal Marines, boarded ships, refuelled at sea, navigated and attended to the thousand and one things that a naval officer might have to do some day. I was also made the official ship's tour guide. Should we pass a Greek island or a volcano, I was sent for and had to broadcast 'interesting facts' to the 2,000-odd souls on board.

I passed my Fleet Board, despite the fact that all the questions were based around a Leander Class frigate. I had never been on board a Leander Class frigate. The rest of my time in the ship was spent driving the boats. At the time I just enjoyed it. Later I came to realise just how much experience I had gained, and I was able to use it when handling big ships.

My first 'complement' job was that of Gunnery Officer in HMS *Hardy*, commanded by the marvellous Lieutenant-Commander 'Black Mac' Neil McLeay, who was now on his eighth command. He was reckoned to be the best submarine-chaser in the Fleet at the time, and it was a pleasure to serve under him. The First Lieutenant was a Lieutenant-Commander Peter Hamlyn, to whom I owe a great debt. It was he who taught me the seaman's eye, without which a sailor is but mediocre. He 'took an interest in the lad,' and we have remained friends ever since.

The Captain was not only a top rate sub-hunter but a superb ship-handler as well. *Hardy* was a single screw Type 14 frigate, and he could turn her round in the river off BRNC using only five engine orders, and without the use of an anchor.

One of my jobs on board was to be the Expeditions Officer and to take the sailors for adventure training as far afield as North Wales. A ten-day excursion into the mountains of Snowdonia won us the Navy's Bulawayo Trophy for the best expedition mounted that year. I very much enjoyed taking the men into rough country and teaching them how to survive and be comfortable as well. I also continued with my canoeing, and started trials on the recovery of a man overboard at sea, using such a craft. These trials were to continue in both my next two ships, until the Navy decided upon a different system. Nevertheless we achieved some success in this field.

Towards the end of the year, one of our boilers blew up and we steamed down to Gibraltar on the other to put the ship into refit and transfer across to her sister ship HMS *Russell*. We also had about three months in Gib. and I made many friends there. Over the years I was to visit the Rock from time to time and continue those friendships.

On our return to the UK 'Black Mac' left *Russell*, his ninth command, and retired from the service, much to the regret of many. We were all sorry that he did not achieve promotion to Commander, for no one could have been more deserving. However, it seems that early in his career he must have put a foot wrong somewhere, and the Navy never forgets. He was relieved by another Lieutenant-Commander under whom I served for a further year until it was time for me to move on again.

I had the job of Captain's Secretary and Gunnery Officer. Spending much of my time on the bridge as officer of the watch, I gained invaluable experience of just how to handle a frigate in all conditions and at all speeds. It was a wonderful opportunity, and I made the most of it, being particularly keen on 'playing' with Fast Patrol Boats, with whom we had constant 'battles'. If they could close in and get abaft our beam, then they were deemed to have won. If we could keep them ahead of the beam, then we had won. They were very adept at doing close passes at very high speed (they could go over twice our maximum), and we became adept at hurling a dozen or so potatoes at them, as they passed, from the giant catapult I had constructed.

In both *Hardy* and *Russell* we visited several ports in northern Europe, including Copenhagen and Brussels. I also got the chance to do some motor rallying and managed, with the Cox'n, to win the team prize in the RN/RM competition. I secured the Bulawayo Trophy for the second year, and started rock climbing. For one month I was lent as instructor to the Moray Outward Bound School at Burghead.

I think that at this point it would be well to examine the reasons behind all this extrovert activity that played such an important part in my life then and subsequently, right until the year that I left the Navy. I have always been very aware of my inadequacies as a person, both physically and mentally, and of my great fear of heights. Everything I did then and have done since has been in the vain attempt to conquer this fear and try to acquire some confidence in my abilities.

Next I joined HMS *Blake*, and it was here that I began

to get involved in folk-singing, boxing and field gun (the competition which always opens the Royal Tournament), and won the Bulawayo Trophy for the third year in succession.

Captain Toby OBE was the CO, and Commander Bill Canning, later to win fame and a DSO as Captain of HMS *Broadsword* in the Falklands, was the Commander. These were two men I would follow anywhere. The 'Snakey Blakey', as she was known, was a Lion Class cruiser converted to carry four anti-submarine helicopters and armed with two six-inch guns, two quick-firing three-inch guns and two Sea Cat launchers. Laid down in 1946, right to the end of her days she continually won the Royal Navy Gunnery Trophy, even against the most modern equipment. She was a wonderful ship, and we all loved her.

Before continuing with the story, I must go back a little to the Type Fourteens. Here indeed was a class of ship that I dearly loved. If destroyers are the greyhounds of the seas, then these surely are the whippets. They were exciting to handle, great sea-boats and very uncomfortable – but one got used to that. They were long, slim and wet, under-gunned and beautiful. I include here some verses from some of the songs and poems I wrote about them.

(From 'A Junior Officer's Farewell to his Ship')

I wonder what you feel, small cockle-shell,
I wonder how you suffer, little ship.
You do not live and breathe like me but, in a time apart,
You leave your name and e'en your very soul in us.
When I'm old and thoughts are grey,
My brain is addled with senility,
So will I veer away from fast approaching winds of death
And walk again upon your living decks – as will we all.

(From 'Drive them Down in a Rolling Sea')

Grafton and Pellew were the first to go
(Drive them down in a Type Fourteen),
With Murray and Blackwood soon in tow
(Drive them down in a rolling sea),
Duncan, Malcolm and Palliser
(Drive them down in a Type Fourteen),
No one thought of saving her
(Drive them down in a rolling sea);
Dundas and Keppel without a care
(Drive them down in a Type Fourteen),
Russel and Hardy within a year
(Drive them down in a rolling sea).
So if you've got a craving to
Drive them down in a Type Fourteen,
There's only Exmouth left for you
To drive them down in a rolling sea.

In HMS *Blake* I was given the Top Part of Ship, and my Division had the biggest collection of rapscallions that I have ever had the pleasure to come across. After about three months, however, I got the measure of them, and the Commander remarked that he had not seen one of my men at his assizes for a long time. My Petty Officer and I may have administered a little rough justice at times, but the boys reacted well and were soon my pride and joy.

As Sports Officer, in charge of all the recreation in the ship, I was required to take away an Exped. almost every week-end, train the men in survival and organise all sports. That year the ship's team came second in the RN Football Championships, the first time in twenty years that a unit of the Fleet had reached the final.

I was invited to help the Portsmouth Area PT Officer host the Navy vs. Army Boxing Tournament, which I agreed to do. Up to that time I had had no interest in boxing at all. However, I was appalled at the condescending attitude displayed towards the event and the contestants, all of whom were ratings, by the officers, and determined that I would put matters right by learning to box myself and entering the first available competition, that all might see that officers did box and were not afraid to get into the ring. Consequently I asked the POGI (Petty Officer Gunnery Instructor), who was the current Navy middleweight champion, to teach me to box. He taught me the basics, and we had three rounds of sparring. I ended up in the RN hospital with two broken ribs and a punctured kidney. When asked why he had caused me these injuries, the GI, Petty Officer Buck Taylor, said, 'Well, he kept hitting me harder and harder, so I just did the same.'

Apart from getting to know well the many Field Gunners that we had on board (five times over the years I was asked by either Portsmouth or Plymouth teams to be their Field Gun Officer, an unusual accolade that I was sadly never able to take up), I also got to know Petty Officer Shep Woolley. A year or so later he left the Navy to take up full-time his budding career as a folk singer and entertainer. We have remained friends ever since, and it was with his encouragement that I started on my own in the same field. I did not play an instrument but sang unaccompanied and started to write my own compositions. Later Shep was to record my song 'The Lament to the Passing of the Montague Whaler'. It is one of his favourite pieces.

'The Lament to the Passing of The Montague Whaler'

Your lacings are frayed and your sheets disarrayed,
Your traveller's jammed at the yard,
You've lost cringle and bung and your planking is sprung
And the grease in your pintle's gone hard.

Your garboard strake's split and your stretchers don't fit,
Your paintwork's beginning to peel,
Your gunn'ls have dipped and your tiller's unshipped
And the dead-wood's adrift from your keel.

They once sailed you proud, sang your praises out loud,
The pride of the ships that you served,
But no more will they shout as they put you about.
Is this the reward you deserved?

For your legend's been told by the sailors of old,
Of the lives that you saved from the sea.
You're the last galliot, you've been left here to rot.
Now who's going to save you for me?

When you shake out your reef, take the wind by its teeth,
And sail into history and song,
Though we've thrown you away, please recall what I say.
Forgive us for being so wrong.

So away with your keelson, away with your yard,
Away with your mizzen and main,
For the days of the Montague Whaler
Are the days we shall not see again.

Each year since leaving Dartmouth I had been told that after 'another year' I would be put on the Clearance Divers course. By now I was at my five-year break-point and quite ready to leave the Navy, having been worked to my utmost capacity in common with most junior officers. At last, now I was offered the course for real. But they had in the past cried wolf too often, and I had lost interest. However, my Exped. activities had caused someone to sit up and take notice, and I was offered a three years Instructor's posting to the Joint Services Mountain Training Centre at Tywyn in North Wales and a transfer to the PT Branch, normally reserved for ex-lower-deck officers. Naturally I jumped at the chance, and prepared to leave the 'Snakey Blakey'.

Captain Toby, in my farewell interview, paid me the ultimate compliment by asking if I would come with him to his next job as one of his personal staff. I thanked him and said that I would have been delighted, but that exciting things were looming on the lee-side of the year and that I therefore had to decline.

I went to Tywyn as the first of a long line of Naval Instructors and thoroughly enjoyed myself there, teaching the young men of the services mountaineering, rock climbing, canoeing, caving, survival and leadership. I was in my element. It was too good to last, though. I had been conned, for, having signed on for another five years, after six months in the job and despite letters written to the Admiralty by the Brigadier Commandant, I was drafted to HMS *Bulwark* as the Damage Control Officer, a dead-end job in a ship where I seemed to be about the only junior officer who was not under Admiralty Warning.

I joined HMS *Bulwark,* then in refit in Devonport, and took over my duties. Soon there came news that I had been selected for the Joint Services Himalayan Expedition to climb Nanda Dahvi. I was delighted, the Commander was not and my Appointer, for once friendly, arranged for my relief to join the ship and for me to be given leave to take part in this opportunity. I joined the expedition training camp, and was then told that there had been a mistake and that I would not be able to go after all. Actually it was just as well. After the first few days' training, both Tug Wilson (then the Navy's number one mountaineer) and I had agreed that, unless the organisation improved dramatically, neither of us was prepared to take part. When I received the news that I was not to be included, Tug (who remains a close friend to this day) declared that he wanted no part of it either, and left with me. As it turned out, the expedition was not a success and the leader lost his life.

I rang my Appointer to tell him the news, and he replied that he had got me on the Clearance Divers course starting shortly at *Vernon*, that I should return to my ship, pack my bags and report to the said establishment. I immediately put this plan into effect; but when I reported to the Commander to say goodbye, the man informed me that he considered I had been underhand, and that he had cancelled my course. I pointed out that this was my last chance to take it and still give the required return of service, and that I wished to see the Captain. He replied that, if I did that, I should not get an extension of service to allow me to get on the next course, since he was the one who wrote my reports. I was conned again – conned and blackmailed.

Despite these rather unsavoury happenings, I had an absolutely marvellous commission in *Bulwark*. We had two deployments to the Mediterranean and one to the Caribbean. The 'Rusty B', as the ship was known, was a sister ship to HMS *Albion* and had the same role. I was in charge of all fire-fighting and damage control and completed the Long Course to become a Fleet NBCD Officer. By now I was a mid-seniority Lieutenant and well versed in my job. The ship carried about 250 officers, and the wardroom was extremely lively. Normally an aircraft-carrier of that size averaged one fire a week, but by unusual and unorthodox means I managed to get the fire-prevention message across and during my time we had no fires. This being the case, I can rate my effectiveness on board as satisfactory, and I look back with pride that the pervading standard of knowledge in all matters connected with my department was higher than in most other ships in the Fleet.

There is not room for me to describe here in detail all the adventures in which I took part. Suffice it to say that I achieved the following:

– Ocean Navigation Certificate;
– I boxed for the ship (and had my nose broken twice);
– the song-writing began to take off;
– I had a splendid 'jug band', which was very popular with the ship's company (76 concerts) and went by the name

of The Malawi International Airways String Quartet
(there were seven of us): we played at the Malta
International Folk Festival, the Grand Bazaar in
Istanbul and the Governor of the Bahamas' Summer
Ball;
– I made enduring friendships with two men, Dick Barr
and Jim Jennings (the Fiddler), which would ultimately
determine the direction that my life was to take.

Leaving *Bulwark* and her splendid Captain, Johnny
Johnson, I was appointed to the Long Mine Clearance
Diving Course at HMS *Vernon*. For a year, under the
watchful eyes of my old friend Chief Clearance Diver Joe
Maher, we were put through the mill in what is perhaps
the most complete diving and mine warfare course in the
world. Both physically and mentally it was extremely
demanding: for obvious reasons I can say no more than
this. I passed out at the end of 1976 and was given the
appointment of First Lieutenant of HMS *Gavinton* under
the brilliant Lieutenant-Commander Robbie Kerr.
Although he was a difficult man to work for at times,
between us we took 'Gavvie' and put her up on a pedestal,
higher than any MCMV has reached before or since. We
broke the existing record for extended time on task mine-
hunting, raising it from 55 hours to 195 hours in one jump,
and then to 278 hours in the next. Much of the existing
guidance in the books of reference had to be rewritten, and
the *Gavinton* became a byword for excellence.

    (From '*Gavinton* Gets There')

    If you want to stay on task,
    Then you've only got to ask
    The *Gavinton* to show you how it's done.
    She's been there the longest yet;
    As a record I will bet
    She will stay renowned the longest on-task 'Ton'.

During my time in Portsmouth while on course, I had been accepted as a member of the Royal Navy boxing squad. Now, from *Gavinton*, I led a team of five young men, myself included, to the RN Scotland Boxing Championships. Despite the shore establishments' entries of up to 35 boxers per team, the 'Gavvies' fought their way to the top, only losing the Championship outright by one point, and that because AB Garry Abnett was not allowed to contest his final owing to a fractured hand. There was the legend born and the word was out: 'Gavvie the Giant-Killers' were on the loose. I won the Open Light-Middleweight Championship and the boys took Featherweight and Light-Heavy. Over the next year and a half, *Gavinton* boxers took nine championship medals. My personal 'finest hour' came when I drove from Rosyth to Portsmouth in seven hours and twenty-three minutes, through freezing fog, to contest the Royal Navy Open Championship with Nickie Croombes, the then European and Commonwealth silver medallist and considered to be the most dangerous man on the circuit. He beat me, of course, but we had the crowd on its feet and cheering us all the way to the dressing-room. It was the finest night of my life and a cracking fight; all the better since I was the official representative of Flag Officer Scotland at the time, and represented him from *inside* the ring. Very Senior officers were most congratulatory, and I knew that at last, after so many years of trying, I had proved the point that officers can box, and box with the best.

(From 'Light-Heavy')

The ring, the battleground you use,
Is empty, shining; win or lose,
With blood of contest, now or then,
It stands for use by special men
Where most would never dare.

I retired then. After all, I was 32 and well past boxing age. Indeed, when I started at age 27 many people said I was a fool; that I could not start two years after the age when most people withdraw from the ring. Well, maybe I was too old, but I fought against the best and gave of my best. No one said I was a fool after that.

Interestingly enough, I understand that my story is retold when the Navy boxing squad are being taught examples of 'dedication' to the sport. Since that time, until my retirement from the RN, I kept very close links with the squad, and used to coach the new members (I qualified as Coach in 1976), support the squad at various venues and act as team manager on occasion. Since the Falklands and the Red Sea clearance I have been guest of honour at two highly prestigious boxing dinners, in London and Newcastle, when the Navy were performing.

Robbie Kerr was a workaholic and demanded more and more of his ship's company, and I was the man to extract it from them. I have never worked so hard nor, at times, so unhappily as I did then. I lost weight and my beard turned grey, but still we achieved ever greater things. Eventually I decided that I had had enough, and wrote a personal and confidential letter to my Appointer asking for advice. He had said that I might, if ever things got muddled. He never replied, but passed my letter upwards until it got to the very top. It then descended down the Fleet chain until it landed upon my Captain's desk. So much for believing what Senior Officers say to you! I was mortified that the man should have done such a thing without a word to me. The result of this piece of underhand treatment was that I lost the plum job that I had been promised, running the new Diving School for the Sultan of Oman's Navy, and was sent to cool my heels for a year on the tiny island of Diego Garcia in the middle of the Indian Ocean, a thousand miles from the nearest continent. Penal servitude.

Before that happened, however, the Captain left and was

relieved by the ex-Clearance Diver, Lieutenant Bob Pilling. He was a splendid man, in his last job in the Navy, who greatly benefited from the legacy left behind by Robbie Kerr. The ship reached higher than ever. Between us we not only achieved great things, but we did so in a relaxed although thoroughly professional way. I vowed then and there that, if ever I was given command, I would do it Bob's way.

I left 'Gavvie' with a tear in my eye and an ache in my heart, for one can get to love a ship no matter what the circumstances. The boys were tremendous, and above all fun, and under Bob Pilling the punishment return was nil.

In Diego Garcia I had the job of First Lieutenant of the Naval Party and Chief of Police for the 2,000 Americans stationed on the island. I also headed up Customs. American servicemen have a great liking for drugs, and these are forbidden under British law. As a consequence, the regulations we enforced were about the toughest anywhere. So thorough were our searches that $30 worth of 'pot' in the Philippines would fetch $3,000 on the island – if you could get it in.

Upon arrival in Diego, the original tropical paradise, I found that I was 'required' to box in the British Indian Ocean Championships in order to uphold the position of the 20 British servicemen there. I fought an American Construction Battalion sailor/steelworker who was 11 inches shorter, 11 pounds heavier and 11 years younger than I, and very handy. I won, but it was a very hard fight and I have not boxed since.

I now spent my leisure time writing songs, teaching myself to play the fiddle, sailing and presenting the 'Fred from Devon Show' on American Forces Radio. I took station leave in Hong Kong for ten days, and altogether enjoyed life fully. It is one of the best years I can remember.

(From 'A Traveller's Dream of Devon', written in Diego Garcia)

And now, though half the world between us surely lies,
A day is never passing but my mind to Devon flies.
If I perchance am homesick, caught a-luff, becalmed, in stays,
Then let me languish under that strange illness all my days.
Oh Devon, far away, where every road must go;
The places where the music will enliven every heart;
Where the friendship of a few means more than they will know,
Where journeys have their ending but where all of mine must start.

At this time the Americans were trying to free hostages held in Iran, and Diego Garcia was the forward support base for their fleet in the Indian Ocean. From an average of two planes a week, by the end of the year we were handling two Galaxy Starlifters and three smaller transports every day. Things were hotting up in the Gulf area.

For my next job, I was sent to the Sultan of Oman's Navy to command *SNV Al Mujahid*, a 35-metre Patrol Boat.

Shortly after my arrival the Iran-Iraq war started in the Gulf, and we spent long days eyeball to eyeball with the belligerent Iranian Navy, keeping the Straits of Hormuz (Omani waters) open for ships to use 'upon their lawful occasions'. It was a fine and exciting job for a young naval officer, requiring flair and panache and a high level of expertise and confidence. We chased 40-knot smugglers with our 28-knot boats, at night, in the dark with no lights or radar, at speed and all within 200 yards of the cliffs: and we caught them. We turned Iranian FPBs back to their own waters with never a shot fired. We practised attack and defence with each other until we learned every variation, and got to know every inch of our own waters. We exercised with the Royal Navy, who beat us in open water but who lost at our inshore game. Above all we patrolled endlessly the entrance to the Gulf and kept safe passage for all.

One day we boarded a fishing boat and found four-and-a-half tons of smuggled silver ingots on board. That was a nice boost for the ship's company. The Omani Junood (sailors) were a wonderful bunch, totally loyal and great fun. I was lucky enough to have as my First Lieutenant Raaees Bahriyya Sayid Shihab bin Tariq bin Taimur al Said. He is a prince of the small royal family and cousin to the Sultan. I rated him very highly as a naval officer, and he has remained a friend to this day. Some of my RN contemporaries in that small band have stayed on in the SON and risen to high rank. We were the last of a short line of RN officers who helped out and trained the Omanis until their own officers were experienced enough to take command themselves and keep the Straits open. This they have done ever since, and it is a measure of their expertise when one realises that, in all that long war, not a single major 'incident' happened in their waters: waters that were the most attractive of all to the enemy.

Shortly after I returned to the UK, I was sent for by the Admiralty and asked to lead a special group of divers that were being sent to the Falklands conflict. I put my affairs in order and collected my men together. Before long we found ourselves en route for Ascension Island in the noisy and cold belly of an RAF Hercules transport, with the minimum gear and a great feeling of adventure and release. We transferred to *RFA Sir Bedivere* and continued on to the South Atlantic, arriving in San Carlos Water before dawn, the only light being the burning HMS *Antelope*. Daylight in 'Bomb Alley' was full of bombs and bombers, tracer and missiles, and helicopters hovering in shelter. Straight away *Sir Bedivere*, *Sir Lancelot* and *Sir Galahad* were hit, as the Argentinians came in to attack from an entirely unexpected angle. My controller asked me if I would consider removing the unexploded bomb in *Galahad*, as to attempt to defuse it was taboo after the *Antelope* disaster. I agreed, and set off with the small group I had chosen to do the job. This had to be undertaken at night since the days were full of attacks.

It would take too long to detail the operation here. However, I can say that we managed to remove the device (live) in eight-and-a-half hours, and the one in *Lancelot*, after she had been grazed by another bomb, in 22 hours non-stop.

Meanwhile my team had been moved ashore to the hospital area at Red Beach, where we were immediately bombed. We dealt with these devices too, and in daylight hours dived on the *Antelope* in order to reduce the height of the wreck.

My men were superb, and not only did they do their job and more, but they helped in the hospital and became stretcher-bearers and orderlies. Whatever was going on my divers, aged between 18 and 25, were there doing it. I do not believe that I could have been in the company of finer men.

A great deal has been written about the Falklands, and we are all well aware of the happenings. My small team were also the first to reboard *RFAs Tristram* and *Galahad* at Bluff Cove. We put out the fires in *Tristram* and explosively opened the stern loading door so that her cargo of much needed ammunition could be removed. We were not able to do a great deal on board *Galahad* as she was still exploding, but we managed to salvage some of her gear. So we did prove useful.

Later on I recovered the last sea mine swept by our forces, and removed it to Fitzroy Sound where we beached it and defused it. This was an interesting task, as the weapon was totally unknown and believed to be fitted with anti-stripping devices.

Unfortunately we did not have the five boxes of special tools that are required for such a job, so with the materials to hand, explosives and long pieces of string, I managed to effect a complete Render Safe Procedure in about two-and-a-half hours. The mine is now in the *Vernon* museum. It is interesting to note that this was the first unknown enemy mine to be defused by hand since Korea.

As to awards for this operation, my Chief Petty Officer was given the Distinguished Service Medal for the *Lancelot* bomb, three of my Leading Hands received Mentions in Dispatches for gallantry, as did our youngest diver, and six of the team were given Commander-in-Chief's Commendations for Bravery. I brought every one of them back, despite having nearly lost half the team in the air raid on the hospital, but within two months of our return two of them had been killed – innocent victims of other people's dangerous driving.

Of course, when the war was over the press had a fieldday with the various stories. They particularly latched on to the fact that we had used a rubber boat full of cornflakes packets to cradle the *Galahad* bomb while we floated it away from the ship; also the fact that I played my fiddle on the odd occasion, including once from the top of a landing-craft after an air raid, cruising among the Fleet anchored in San Carlos Water. I suppose that one had to expect the press to be that way; although why they could not report the important things others did, I do not know. Perhaps they have got their values mixed up. The 'Falklands Fiddle', however, is now in the Royal Marines Museum at Eastney.

The artist John Lawyer painted three very fine pictures of my team's doings, one of which (a copy) I decided to give to Wellington. I have since been informed that it is hanging in the passage outside the Master's study.

I returned to the UK to become the Explosive Ordnance Disposal Officer to Flag Officer Plymouth. This was an excellent job, covering about a third of the country and involving anything explosive, from Second World War sea mines to hand-grenades found in back gardens and terrorist bombs (car-, letter- or otherwise). I was in my element and also had a chance to work with many of the friends I had made in the Special Forces, with whom we had shared *RFA Sir Lancelot* in the Falklands.

During this period I was becoming concerned about my future. My time was nearly up, and despite many recommendations for promotion and extension I remained a Lieutenant; the most senior Lieutenant in the Navy with twelve years' seniority, the pay increments stopping after six. I went to see the Director of Naval Officers' Appointing and asked him, 'Just how much do I have to do to be promoted and allowed to sign on?' He did not have an answer although he did talk for a considerable time. The result was that I was promoted and signed on, though somewhat late in the day.

I was appointed in command of HMS *Brinton*. While on a brief course at *Vernon*, I met Paul Bootherstone, now Captain, previously my CO in *Brinton*. When I told him that his Mid was about to command his old ship, he was delighted. However, suddenly the captain of HMS *Gavinton* had to leave his ship and my appointment was changed to command her. They say, 'Never go back.' I wondered how right they would be.

I joined her out in the Med, where a squadron of these ships was standing by to react to any mine threat in the Gulf. I found it a great pleasure to be back and set about running the ship as I had vowed that I would all those years ago. Soon, though, we were ordered to the Gulf of Suez where, in that year of 1984, mines had been laid and ships had been damaged. We were part of an international effort to sweep and hunt those waters clear of mines. Again I put my affairs in order and set off to war, this time in the belief that the chances of coming back were not good. Mine-hunting is a hazardous sport.

For three months we hunted and at the end we could give a positive assurance that there were no mines in our area. We, the RN, had found two and we, *Gavinton*, had been the ship responsible in both cases. One was a beautifully preserved and still lethal Second World War German magnetic mine, which we blew up with great delight. The other was an unknown type of Russian ground mine, only the second unknown 'enemy' mine to be found and defused since Korea. The man who defused it, Warrant Officer Diver Terry Seatle, received the Queen's

Gallantry Medal. I was later told that my First Lieutenant, the excellent Robin Swaine, and I are the only officers in the Royal Navy to have successfully hunted a live mine 'in anger'.

The squadron returned to England amid quiet rejoicing. Some time after we were informed that the commander of the squadron had been made OBE and the two captains of ships connected with the finding and disposal of the 'new' mine, myself and Grenville Johnson, had been made MBE. It was not until 1988, six years later, that all the men in the ships were to be awarded a special clasp to the General Service Medal for their part in the clearance.

I remained in command of HMS *Gavinton* for two-and-a-bit years, and had a splendid succession of young officers working under me. My ship's company were mustard too, and the punishment returns were consistently nil. We achieved a reputation for excellence such as the ship had before, and I was able to use my experiences in Oman to enhance the tactical expertise of the squadron. I think that we were all touched by the 'Gavvie Magic' and had a happy time on board. 'It's great to be a Gavvie!' the boys used to say, and so it was. Many of them still keep in touch, and one young seaman has since won the Queen's Sword at Dartmouth as the best Sub-Lieutenant of his year. Two of my officers now command their own ships and our squadron commander, Anthony Chilton OBE, is now the commander of the Royal Yacht (since appointed as the last Commodore of the Royal Naval College at Greenwich). Eventually, after over two years of commission, we safely brought the ship into Rosyth for the last time and paid her off into reserve. She now sits at a buoy in Portsmouth, waiting 'to die the lonely death of the ship that men forgot'.

> For you're dying, my friend, and the life that we lend
> Can only prolong your demise;
> So perhaps you should go where all faithful ships go,
> And sail ever more 'neath blue skies.

(And from 'The Old Tin Gear' – slang for minesweeping gear)

> The crew are on the sweep-deck, life-jackets on their backs,
> There's wire and poles and tins of grease, a cropper and an axe;
> The sweep is out, the kite is down, the cutters are all set;
> The tea is made – 'Come quickly, lads, we've just time for a wet.'
>
> There's Paddy, Taff and Nobby there, Young 'Arry's helping too;
> In all Rosyth you'll never find a better sweep-deck crew.
> The wire is in, the gear is stowed, the course we set is west;
> But for finding mines, it must be said that sonar is the best.
>
> For now I've got my hook up,
> There's nothing that I fear;
> I'm the gaffer of the lads that stream
> The old tin gear.

[Note: a hook (anchor) on the sleeve of a uniform signifies a Leading Hand.]

I now went back to the Falklands for a few months to wind up the Clearance Diving team there, and found the place much changed. Perhaps the saddest thing is that, on a group of islands that once had a musical tradition equal to that of the Shetlands, there is now only one man who plays music and not a single child is learning to play an instrument.

After returning to the UK, I was asked to start up a special team of divers, to be used in unusual and potentially high-risk situations. This was a wonderful opportunity for me since, given my age and seniority, I should by now have started on the normal round of desk jobs. However, owing to my past experience it was considered that I was the ideal man for the job. So for the next year-and-a-half I commanded the finest men that the Navy had to offer. From parachuting to attack swimming to bomb-disposal, we did the lot. Never was there such a highly qualified team. This was indeed the pinnacle of my career.

Years ago I said that I wanted to be 'a recognised expert in my own field'. I achieved that after the Falklands conflict when I received an invitation from the exclusive and highly prestigious Institute of Explosive Engineers to become a Member. Three bomb-disposal men from that time were thus honoured – two DSCs and a DSO.

The next aim that I had was to command one of Her Majesty's Ships, and this too I achieved with the dear old *Gavinton*, 33 years a front line MCMV, of whom I was the last captain.

Now that I was commanding the flower of the Naval Diving Branch, what else could there be? It is unfortunate that someone with my sort of history never gets very far in peacetime. People look at one as some kind of oddity, and to carry six medal ribbons on one's left breast is to invite jealousy and disdain. I decided that now was a good time to go. Remembering the advice given to me so long ago by David Gordon, 'Leave them clapping', I applied for early retirement and got myself a job as Ratings Training Officer in the Sultan of Oman's Navy. I am now back with those splendid Junood in the country that I like so well.

There you have a brief but rambling history, which I hope may amuse and enlighten you. I wish you a very happy retirement, and leave you with this parting verse.

(From 'Farewell the Ship')

So though they scatter all your bones
To four majestic winds and seven seas,
Your name and selfless canopy will e'er remain
With those you've sheltered in your lee.

You cannot be destroyed or left unknown,
You cannot be forgotten or outcast;
For old men talk and, when they walk no more,
Remember love they gave thee to the last.

Since writing this letter, and having designed/built my own yacht to sail back to the UK, I was offered the exciting prospect of becoming Sailing Master of the Sultan of Oman's sail-training tall-ship, the square-rig barquentine Shabab Oman. This internationally renowned ship made two mammoth voyages in the five years I was on board, visiting Rouen in France and later St Petersburg in Russia. Here she became the first non-European ship to win the coveted and prestigious Cutty Sark Trophy for best fostering international relations between young people. As a parting gesture of thanks, and a fitting end to my naval career, I was promoted to Commander – the same rank as my father held before me. (Shabab Oman, under the inspired captaincy of Commander Chris Biggins, has since gone on to win the Cutty Sark Trophy for an unprecedented second time. Such is the stamp of men I have been fortunate to serve under and work with.)

APPENDIX 5

The Notebook

'I wouldn't have your job, mate!'
(another popular saying of the time)

(*Reproduced here as it was written, the Notebook provides an interesting enhancement to the main narrative of Chapters 1 to 3.*)

Announcement made over the Tanoy System on board *RFA Sir Lancelot*
'D'y hear there! For those of the SAS expecting helicopters today – don't, coz there ain't none – no more – until tomorrow – maybe!'

Notice in *Lancelot* Wardroom:-
Until further notice RIG is relaxed in the bar and saloon to anything clean which will not damage the furnishings.
         CHOFF (Chief Officer)

(Message to the crewman of *Wessex* bringing us back from Bluff Cove (*Sir T* and *Sir G*))
'Would you like one of us to come back with you to hook on the load? That is no problem and we would be happy to oblige.'
and
'When we left Red Beach the Team was still there but moving to L. If our gear has gone from RB [Red Beach] we go to *Lancelot*.'

(*Notes made as reminders prior to leaving*)
The 'going outside' signal. How long do those due out have to remain?
Explosives ready!
Dental appointment (important) for L/D Kearns (Bad)

FALKLAND ISLES
(ANON)

IT'S COLD WIND, THE WEST WIND
FULL OF ARGIES' CRIES
I NEVER HEAR THE WEST WIND
FOR THE HAND THAT COVERS MINE EYES
IT COMES FROM PORT STANLEY,
TWIN SISTERS TOO.
DEATH IS IN THE WEST WIND
AND VICTORY TOO.

(Found in Red Beach Command Post)

Also, 'Please do not ask me to do anything when it's *RED*!'

Do you remember the Falklands?

I remember:-
Red Beach One at Ajax Bay.
    Exeter taking out a camberra during breakfast with Sea Dart. 15 miles, 33,000 ft.
    John Boy getting terribly ill.
    Wheels working in the theatre, holding clamps so the Doc could stitch up his incision.
    The shuffling feet of the 20 man lines of Argy prisoners, bootlaceless and right hand on shoulder of man in front.
    The stink of them.
    Mealtimes at dawn and dusk. A dollop of stew and a dollop of potato and away you go.
    The black mud that got everywhere, especially sticking to

the toecap and welt of your boot.

Chief Fox's answer to an inquiry after a long gash on his shin, 'Sangar rash!'

The helos bringing in casualties and the lads doing stretcher party/nurse/orderly.

Compo.

Seeing the belly of the plane that bombed *Sir Galahad* and the splash of one of its bombs.

The stink of a burning ship.

A young lad left in sole possession of the upper deck of *Sir G*.

How the booze flowed. Always there seemed to be a tot handy.

The Falkland Farewell: 'See you. Keep your head down.'

Young Joe Gofton who seemed to have a smile ready for any occasion.

Tommo and Whiskey festooned in m/g bullets and smgs [sub-machine-guns] having their 'bad' photo taken.

A cold night in *Sir Tristram*.

A mess full of Armalites and strange SAS kit. Bullets everywhere.

'Flying' in a Rigid Raider.

The way the lads worked to build the sandbag blast wall.

Wet gravel down your neck.

A frightened Argy Pilot.

How the Colonel from Goose Green spilled his secrets after witnessing an 'op' on one Argy.

Padre from *Cardiff* claims 1 Skyhawk shot down by Sea Dart at 32 miles and 38,000 ft (on Sunday night!!)

Sitting Duck Creek (SDC), part of Bomb Alley, where the LSLs got zapped in San Carlos Water.

The Mirage Pilot who, seeing *Fearless*'s Sea-Cat gaining on him, ejected 5 secs before the missile ran out of fuel and fell to the ground.

My personal bomb shelter at Red Beach. The piss-place by the corner of the building by Fort Thompson. (I tried a sangar once but did not like it at all. Preferred the open air.)

Rose Cottage, the tent in Fort Thompson.

The Heads tent, complete with straining-bars, dug by FCDT 3.

Lying in the bottom of an LCVP while rockets, jets and shrapnel passed close overhead.

The jubilation of a Marine when he hit a Skyhawk with his SLR.

A surviving stoker from *Plymouth* waiting for an operation and his concern for his oppo wounded in the head.

The dolphin that led our Gemini round to Green Beach.

Dawn breaking over the Ships in the Sound.

Trying to find *Fearless* in the dark, one flat calm morning, and coming across a ghostlike *Canberra*, the sole ship in.

The sleep in *Intrepid* in an LCU, on a pile of baggage after the *Galahad* job and the sheer bliss of soaking my hands in hot water.

Playing fiddle on the way past *Fearless*, from the bridge roof of an LCU, just after an air raid and how they clapped and cheered.

Tommo's Jacques Cousteau impression.

The bomb crease in the side of *Lancelot* and the damage to the galley within.

Continually meeting old friends.

The bitter wind from Stanley.

Watching *Antelope* burn, break and, after the bow rising taut from the water, finally subside.

Brian Dutton heading fast for the Gemini on hearing an Air Raid Red in *Argonaut*, and me following. That was the first day.

Glamorgan, hit by an Exocet, but seemingly not too badly damaged. Her own fault for cutting the corner of the danger zone. Same team as ran her aground at Muscat some weeks before!

Commander Jolly who headed up the Medical Team. 'Welcome to the Red and Green Life Machine.'

The CP sangar; always seemed to be the same people on

watch. Warm in there.

The pain of 'trench foot' after days spent in sea boots.

The burn cases from Goose Green.

The Chinese survivors from *Sir Galahad* who slept in half of our mess.

Scrambling through the burned out superstructure of *Sir Tristram*, and blowing the back door off her.

How the *Lancelot* bomb slipped, jerked and did not explode.

The Gemini full of cornflakes packets into which we lowered the *Galahad* bomb.

Seeing myself on TV after the interview and the way the reporters were rapt with attention.

The greeting Piggy and I got from the Captain of *Fearless* when we gave him the Antelope plaque.

Feeding a burn casualty.

A funeral on the bleak South Ridge where we buried 4 airmen in a common grave, and 'The Dark Isle'. And still the helos came.

The bomb that passed through *Bedivere*'s mast, crane and FX bulwark.

The state of HMS *Cardiff* when she came alongside and the amount of burned/missing paint.

A peaceful morning in San Carlos Water after the surrender, calm and windless, watching the sun rise.

The Booties dug in on North Ridge. After 2 × Argy Bombs blown up and 3 × bits of RN ordinance, they asked us to tell the *Exeter* that they were friendly and to stop throwing things at them.

A hot shower in *Fearless*.

The Percy Pongo who found a bomb and no one would believe him – but it was there.

The Royal who tried to extract this parachute hanging out of the wall, to take home as a rabbit ('gizzit'), only to find a 500 lb bomb on the other end.

Joe Gofton trying to play harmonica.

The rattle of small arms fire during air attacks and the red flare of a 'blowpipe' missile chasing a Mirage jet.

A Volvo tractor/trailer quietly tracking through the black, peaty mud.

The Eager-Beavers constantly at work shifting stores and the sound of their engines.

Three generators chugging away outside the Medical Facility.

The food queue before the bombs. The desolation of the blast area afterwards.

Negative flies.

Night in the Naval Mess. Hammocks, camp beds and half-heard music escaping from head-sets.

Tommo, Wheels and Phil constantly writing letters.

The door into the big building at Red Beach that you had to shoulder-charge to open.

A bomb at the water's edge. Another on North Ridge.

Reports of looting in *Fearless* and *Intrepid* by the Scots and Welsh Guards.

12 boxes of phosphorus grenades we got off the *Sir Galahad*.

My poncho that did good service – until nicked by someone.

Bad feet.

A Shag on the jetty cleaning himself.

Picnicking on *Sir L*'s bridge during the cold-move to safer anchorage.

Cardiff's Padre stating that they had shot down 3 aircraft and the Choff of L's answer, 'Really? We've shot down five.'

Seeing *Plymouth* with a large patch on her funnel. She had 4 bombs pass through her!

Fearless lying across the sound with her Sea Cats pointing 8 to SE, 8 to NE during a 'Red.'

A Mirage heading fast towards the ridge to the south, hotly pursued by a Rapier. He did not make it.

Small wooden 'stools' used for anything from desk to seat to table. Where did they come from? (Red Beach).

A cold, wet morning trip to Green Beach and back in an LCU during a Bombardment Alert.

Getting the plaque off the bridge-front of *Sir T* for the Captain, who had nothing left.

The Choff of *Sir G* leaving with his Survival Pack.

A Commander Engineer getting in our way everywhere. Keen, but seemingly out of depth.

Chief Siddle cutting away the stair well above the *Sir L* bomb.

Picking at a bomb fuse with a toothpick while upside down (me).

Sitting on the deck in acid with a bomb and wrapped-around sheet of alloy, partially resting on my knees.

Whiskey and Buster and the 'Big Bad Bomb.'

'Red Alert lads; put your boots on but no need to get up.' 'But it's 5 o'clock in the morning!'

My corner of the Red Beach mess.

Seeing a few sheep. Where are the rest?

Taff Hurley and the body-bag spoof.

Burned fighting order. Burned guns. Burned bayonets. (*Sir G*)

An LCVP on the rocks.

Rum.

Members of FCDT 2 accused of looting on board. (*Sir L*)

Giving all the team's spare clothes to half-naked Bluff Cove survivors.

The captured Argy guns and bayonets and helmets that the SAS brought back in great numbers.

The boredom of being on board *Sir L* and no task to do.

Running out of blue (beer) and only green (lager) to drink. Mr Shoo, the barman in *Sir L*.

The jawbones of a Whale at Port San Carlos.

Sheep corals made of grown gorse.

The Harrier Strip at Green Beach.

My lads digging a latrine.

Fresh eggs on Red Beach and the Chef's 'object' on the wall with the message 'Yes, this *IS* an egg!' And his bracken fronds decorating the structure. And playing for the dinner queue.

The red 'Red' whistle hanging at the CP and the sound of it: 6 short blasts.

The long blast of the 'Yellow' and the inevitable question: 'Is it yellow?'

Sgt to Sailor (Diver) waiting for casualties. 'It's RED alert!' 'Sorry, too busy to worry about that now.'

Being laid low with flu.

Looting that occurred in *Sir Tristram*.

John Boy's training shoes that he always wore.

Hacking at a bit of compressed wood under a bomb with a knife, saw blade and finally bayonet.

Slinging two bombs.

A 500 lb-er lying in the roof and the other in the refrigeration plant. Two more on North Ridge, two on the beach and another two further out.

The LCU that found one bomb – by sitting on it at low tide!

The LCU cox'ns . Ginge from *Bulwark*. Colin Garwood.

Hot chocolate laced with Rum.

Sleeping bags.

Casualties waiting for operations and how the lads looked after them.

Biscuits fruit – AB.

Upland goose (braised) on the newest Prince's Splicers day. 'To the Heir to the Heir to the Throne.'

'Queens' at Ratings' rum issue.

The acid from *Sir G*, that burned through my combats.

Sangars.

Father John Ryan.

Listening to David Foxley (Captain RE) describing his escape from *Sir Galahad*.

Shell holes in the peat around Twin Sisters and Argie defences.

Playing 'ball' with an Argie contact mine in breaking seas.

Heloing onto *Cordella* in rough seas. Lots of movements on the ship and swing on the winch.

'Tough-as-Teak' Tex Marshall.

Removing the det from the Mean Mad Machine (Argy mine).

Sharing a pair of my epaulettes with Alex Manning (when we started wearing them again). He had right, I had left.

Dophins racing the Gemini.

The Mine looking menacing and just as everyone expects it to be, either floating in the water with horns uppermost or on *Junella*'s Sweep Deck.

Aunt Vi at the Pettersons. Playing fiddle in their kitchen.

The multi colours of the Stanley houses and the mud in the streets.

Curfew.

Dhobying in *Sir Lancelot* laundry. (Routine: strip off, everything in machine, shower etc, hang around for a bit, extract clothes, get dressed. After Bluff Cove it was all we had.)

Diver the ex-*Endurance* survey boat given to FCDT 3.

The Diving shack perched atop a rotting hulk in Stanley.

The wreck of a barque, 3 masts standing, main yard still crossed.

'Sea lions' in Fitzroy water.

Commodore Amphibious Warfare, 'What are you going to blow up now?'

Belle and Bozo, the Pettersons' dogs.

The cold waters of Fitzroy.

A wardroom full of Staff – like toppers – in *Lancelot*.

Fiddler's letters.

One man's bug eyes and his reaction at first seeing bomb damage.

Piggy Trotter's unfailing good humour.

The surprisingly small size of a Rapier battery.

Guns at Bluff Cove and a deaf eagle.

Johnny Gurkha in Stanley.

How young some of the troops seemed. Perhaps I am getting old. And how about some of the helo pilots?

Welsh Guards on an anti-looting patrol!

A wardroom full of drunk Commanders.

John Boy refusing a Mars bar!

Fred, the SAS Sgt, and the Bo Derek joke. So does he! Tickled pink.

Tommo's 'down' and then his subsequent 'up'.

Meeting Peter Myat from Tutwell on board *Falkland Sound* on a 'jolly' to Kidney Island.

The greater black-backed Fleet Clearance Diver Clearer (killer whale/Leopard seal etc).

Fiddling *Falkland Sound* in on her last trip under Ian Craig's command. Someone, suspect Lt Cdr on *Baltic Ferry*, complained and QHM told us to cool it.

Standing on the 'corner' in Stanley and seeing – Guardsmen saluting everyone, a division of soldiers being inspected in the mud, two lots of men marching three abreast, defaulters doubling in ranks. We looked at each other, Alex and I, turned over badges of rank and said, 'Time to go home!'

Argy guns swung round from the sea to point west to Twin Sisters (at Stanley).

General Moore, 'What's all this about a curfew, Bernie? I never said anything about a curfew.'

'*Hermes, Hermes,* this QHM afloat in *Tiger Bay,* over.'

'QHM afloat in *Tiger Bay,* this is *Hermes,* over.'

'*Hermes, Hermes,* this QHM afloat in *Tiger Bay,* over.'

'QHM afloat in *Tiger Bay,* this is *Hermes,* over.'

'*Hermes,* this is QHM afloat in *Tiger Bay,* you are broken, channel 12 please, over.'

'QHM afloat in *Tiger Bay,* this is *Hermes,* roger channel 12, going down, over.'

'*Hermes, Hermes,* this is QHM afloat in *Tiger Bay,* do you read me, over.'

'QHM afloat in *Tiger Bay,* this is *Hermes.* I read you loud and clear, over.'

'*Hermes,* this is QHM afloat in *Tiger Bay.* Welcome to Port Stanley – over.'

'QHM afloat in *Tiger Bay,* this is *Hermes.* Roger, going back to 16, out.'

And then they did it all over again for the reply: 'Thank you, nice to be here.'

A warehouse full of bales of wool.

Saturday night in the 'Victory Bar', Port Stanley.

The Old Dear and her ex-piper husband to whom I played 'Barren Rocks of Aden' and their oppo, with glasses, who kept shaking my hand.

The sticker behind the bar. 'GOOD 'ERE, INNIT!'

Standing on a chair to play.

Match-games in *Sir B*'s Sgts Mess.

Standing on the poop of *Sir B* with Mark Hare, looking across a snow covered and moonlit Stanley Harbour.

Wheels' 35 letters in one mail drop!

Sitting on a Board of Trade life jacket down the Mess having a can and a chat with the lads.

The lads willing a Herc to land at Stanley, which it did at the 3rd pass, and giving it a round of applause.

3rd Officer 'Tintin' in *Sir Bedivere* and the well-bearded Choff of *Sir Lancelot*.

Negi-water in the LSLs, dhobying everything in a small sink.

The SAS party in Stanley. Cabaret.

General Moore looking every inch the fighting General at the march-past but looking tired in the Wardroom.

Col Sgt Garwood's moustaches and playing his LCU into Green Beach from the jetty.

Liquid mud at Port San Carlos.

My socks being nicked off my pit in the Officers' mess-deck.

The lads trying vainly to start the compressor.

Snow beautifying the hulks and jetties of Stanley.

The RAF camped on the airfield in Tropical Tents!

Young Royal off LCVPs guarding fiddle in the window of the Victory.

The hands of the Bluff Cove burn victims, covered in white ointment and wrapped in plastic bags.

Being the first person to receive a letter and everyone's

envy until we discovered that it was a bill from Gieves!

MODERN NURSERY RHYMES

Twin Sisters, Twin Sisters out beyond the town,
Where were the Argies when the sky fell down?
Up came Johnny Gurkha with his kukri and his gun.
Off went the Argy soldiers – run, run, run!

BB

Goosey, Goosey, Goosey Green,
I think I've found an Argy spleen
Belonging to a spic Marine
Who wished that he had never been
To Goosey, Goosey, Goosey Green.

Anon

Sangary, Sangary, Sangary Rye,
Where will you be when the bombers come by?
Following Piggy, following Dave
Into a sangar my life to save.

BB

BLUFF COVE

The water's cold at Fitzroy,
Cold as a witch's tits;
Damn cold, death cold,
It really gives me the shits!

Tommo
(Mine Recovery Team 26.6.82)

RSP ARGENTINE BUOYANT MINE 27.6.82

Team: Lt N A BRUEN
CPO (D) G TROTTER
LS (D) A THOMPSON
CPO (MW) ROY MARSHALL
LS (MW) NICHOLAS SMITH

Mine swept by HMS *Pict*, taken in tow by HMS *Junella* on 25.6.82 towed to Fitzroy Sound and anchored over night. First 'in water' close recce carried out by Lt Bruen, CPO (MW) Marshall plus LS (MW) Smith by Gemini am 26.6.82. The mine was not recognised by any of the recce team.

PM 26.6.82 CPO (D) Trotter and LS (D) Thompson were flown by helo to *Junella* with all available CBs. CPO (D) plus LS (D) taken to mine by Gemini.

A subsequent search through CBs could not reveal the identification of the mine.

Permission to beach the mine and an RSP [Render Safe Procedure] carried out was given by SMCDO (COMMAW).

A sledge was constructed, consisting of a 45 gallon oil drum cut into two halves (lengthways), a wooden cargo pallet and a life buoy. This was to be used to seat the mine on, in order that none of the Hertz horns be damaged during beaching.

The beaching operation commenced at first light on the 27.6.82. Once this had been achieved the team returned to HMS *Junella* to plan the RSP.

The RSP Plan was as follows:

1) Remove all but 2 nuts from the bottom plate.
2) To blow off the remaining two nuts using explosive, and removing the bottom plate remotely.
3) Usual inspection of bottom of mine once bottom plate removed.
4) To remove remotely a top cover plate and inspect inside this aperture.

TEAM FOR RSP:- LT BRUEN CPO TROTTER LS THOMPSON CPO MARSHALL

The following times were recorded
a) removal of 5 nuts on base plate

	commenced	completed
1st nut	1643	1643.44
2nd nut	1643.50	1644.10
3rd nut	1644.20	1644.50
4th nut	1645.10	1645.25
5th nut	1645.35	1646.15

b) remaining two nuts blown off at 1716 (commenced placing charge) nuts off at 1731.
c) attach cordage and remotely pull off base plate at 1737.
d) inspect bottom of mine.
e) remove centre nut from top plate remotely *commence 1741 complete 1752.*
f) remove top cover remotely *commence 1754 complete 1757.*
g) remove wing nut from suspect detonator placer bottom mine *commenced 1807 completed 1808.*
h) remove inner charge case bung (upper) commence 1809 *unsuccessful.*
i) outer ring upper case bung attempted to remove *commenced 1810 completed 1811* (suspect top of primers – could not be removed).
j) commence removing bung in bottom of charge case (nothing found) *commenced 1823 completed 1827.*
k) detonator removed from detonator placer mechanism.

Mine rendered safe at 1835 by a team with a superb blend of professional knowledge and experience.

[Author's note: Little credence can be given to the timings shown here. CPO Marshall wrote this up the next day. For many of the actions described, it would be impossible to complete them in the time.]

Red Beach Kit

Boots	Pipe
Long Johns	Tobacco
Woolly shirt	Matches
Sweater	Survival kit
Combat trousers	Bayonet
Quilted waistcoat	Survival bag
Wristlettes	Clasp knife
Combat jacket	Arm knife
Headover	Journal, Notebook
Foot cream + powder	Spoon
Hexy stove + fuel	John Wayne (tin opener)
'String'	Mess tin
B + MD hat	Rations
Gloves	Poncho
Calumlights (2)	Water bottle
Pen	Rum flask
Torch	Soap
Heads paper	Toothbrush/paste
Compass	

Survival/Travelling Kit

1 pair boots	Pipe
1 pair shoes/trainers	Tobacco
2 pairs socks	Matches
2 pairs nicks	Wallet
2 vests	Cheque book
2 shirts	Notebook, Journal
2 Jeans/trousers	Fiddle
1 sweater	Sleeping bag
1 waistcoat (quilted)	Carrying bag
1 jacket	Pipe cleaners
1 pair gloves	tooth brush/paste
1 hat	ID card
1 headover	Pen
4 handkerchiefs	Tent
1 belt + knife	Torch

1 set waterproofs
1 neckerchief
Sheath knife
Water bottle
House key
Camera (small)

Mess Traps
Stove
KFS
Rations
Foot powder

Messages collected from friends of Fiddler to take back to him in UK
Do you remember end of Clockwork '72 on board *Sir Geraint*, a Zulu Warrior, a set of Lovats that met with a scuttle? Well . . . . read on:
I know, I was that man
Steve Walsh

You told me how to do it,
Now I'm doing it.
You were wrong.
You did not tell about bangs and flashes.
Teapot

Fiddler
From a sprog Cpl who knew you years ago, now a CSM, I wish I knew you now.
Keith McDonald

Fiddler
From a connoisseur of your fiddling at the 'Plume' ['Plume of Feathers' pub at Princetown on Dartmoor, a favourite place to be]. Hope we meet again soon.
Joe Askwith

Fiddler
Remember the time in the Stonehouse wine and spirit years ago, well some of us are still about. I hope you are well, and next I'm down that way I'll try and look you up.
Colin Garwood

Passwords

231200z – 241200z Short Biscuit
241200 – 251200 Roman Charm
251200 – 261200 Open House
261200 – 271200 Golf Partner
Thereafter they went to the numbers.

The Rose

Auntie Velma Melthan
Uncle George

Norma Porter's Husband

Tony and Heather Pedeson half share

Vivienne Perkins
Victory Bar
Stanley
FI SA

Signal from Ghurkas at Goose Green:
 'Unless we get some rations here soon, you'll have to change the name of this place.'

Endpiece

 We set a sail and see where it takes us.
 We make friends and then we move on.
 All we can do is remember as best we can.

BB.